T0080254

Global Islam: A Very Short Introduction

VERY SHORT INTRODUCTIONS are for anyone wanting a stimulating and accessible way into a new subject. They are written by experts, and have been translated into more than 45 different languages.

The series began in 1995, and now covers a wide variety of topics in every discipline. The VSI library currently contains over 650 volumes—a Very Short Introduction to everything from Psychology and Philosophy of Science to American History and Relativity—and continues to grow in every subject area.

Very Short Introductions available now:

Available soon:

For more information visit our web site

www.oup.com/vsi/

Nile Green

GLOBAL ISLAM

A Very Short Introduction

OXFORD
UNIVERSITY PRESS

Oxford University Press is a department of the University of Oxford.
It furthers the University's objective of excellence in research, scholarship,
and education by publishing worldwide. Oxford is a registered trade mark of
Oxford University Press in the UK and certain other countries.

Published in the United States of America by Oxford University Press
198 Madison Avenue, New York, NY 10016, United States of America.

Library of Congress Cataloging-in-Publication Data

Names: Green, Nile, Author.
Title: Global Islam : a very short introduction / Nile Green.
Description: New York : Oxford University Press, 2020. |
Series: Very short introduction
Identifiers: LCCN 2020024070 (print) | LCCN 2020024071 (ebook) |
ISBN 9780190917234 (paperback) | ISBN 9780190917258 (epub)
Subjects: LCSH: Globalization—Religious aspects—Islam. |
Islam—20th century. | Islam—21st century.
Classification: LCC BP190.5.G56 G74 2020 (print) | LCC BP190.5.G56
(ebook) | DDC 297.09—dc23
LC record available at https://lccn.loc.gov/2020024070
LC ebook record available at https://lccn.loc.gov/2020024071

1 3 5 7 9 8 6 4 2

Printed in Great Britain by Ashford Colour Press Ltd., Gosport, Hants.,
on acid-free paper

The fact is, Islam does move.

Wilfred Scawen Blunt, *The Future of Islam* (Cairo, 1882)

Contents

List of illustrations

Acknowledgments

The writing of this book was supported by a Guggenheim Fellowship and a Luce/ACLS Fellowship in Religion, Journalism & International Affairs from the Henry Luce Foundation and the American Council of Learned Societies. However, the ideas and arguments presented here draw on three decades of travel among Muslim communities worldwide, including India, Pakistan, Iran, Afghanistan, Chinese central Asia, Turkey, Syria, Egypt, Yemen, Saudi Arabia, Oman, Jordan, Morocco, the United Arab Emirates, Sri Lanka, South Africa, Tanzania, Myanmar, Malaysia, Uzbekistan, and Kazakhstan, as well as western and southeastern Europe, the United States, and Japan.

In surveying so many periods and places, I have benefited greatly from reading what has become a vast body of scholarship, comprising scores of books and hundreds of specialist articles. While I have necessarily only listed a sample of books in the Further Reading, I gratefully acknowledge my indebtedness to the many meticulous researchers who have laid the grounds for my general survey.

For comments on previous drafts, I am grateful to Brannon Ingram, Michael O'Sullivan, and Bojan Petrovic, as well as my two anonymous reviewers. Additional thanks go to Anna Heitmann and Michael O'Sullivan for their editorial assistance.

I am also indebted to Don Fehr, my agent at Trident Media, and Nancy Toff, my editor at Oxford University Press, for their encouragement and support. Finally, my sincere thanks to the countless Muslims in so many corners of the world who over the past decades have discussed with me both the delights and dilemmas of our faith.

Introduction

In response to confusing discussions of the impact of Islam around the world, this book addresses two simple questions: what is global Islam, and where did it come from? In other words, this *Very Short Introduction* defines what we might mean by "global Islam," then describes its origins, expansion, and diversification.

As used here, the term "global Islam" refers to the doctrines and practices promoted by transnational religious activists, organizations, and states during the era of modern globalization. The scope of global Islam involves Africa and Asia as much as the Middle East and the West. Yet this book does not make generalizations about the world's entire Muslim population, nor should it be read in that way. Rather, it is a survey of a far smaller cadre of internationally active individuals and organizations, albeit a cadre that, by techniques of persuasion and in some cases coercion, has sought to influence larger numbers of people.

Religious globalization inevitably involves transformation. But as we will see, globalization has not brought about a single, unified Islam. Instead, it has enabled the emergence and proliferation of many different versions of the faith, both political and nonpolitical. To show how this has happened, we will trace the origins, expansion, and increasing diversification of global Islam—from individual activists to organizations and finally to states—that has taken place in tandem with modern globalization since around 1870. In this way, we will answer the deceptively simple question of where global Islam came from. What we will see as a result is not the consolidation of a single Islamic "civilizational bloc," but a more complex kaleidoscope of shifting and competing forms of faith.

Global Islam did not emerge through some innate Muslim tendency toward expansionism. Rather, it came into being through attempts by a variety of actors in the Middle East, Asia, Africa, Europe, even and the Americas to resort to (but often thereby reinvent) religion in order to solve the major problems confronting their communities, whether social, political, moral or existential. In many cases, their motivations came from actual or perceived threats from colonialism, nationalism, socialism, and capitalism, along with the materialist drift of modernization and the cultural pressures of globalization itself.

While some of the new versions of Islam that were formulated in response to these threats were expressly political, many were not. What these new religious visions held in common was their promoters' use of the manifold opportunities offered by globalization to spread their particular solutions to spiritual or political problems. For this reason, rather than focus primarily on the finer points of theology or ritual, this book pays special attention to the crucial mechanisms of communication and organization that allowed some of these new versions of Islam to wield more influence than others, often in places far from their points of origin.

These different models of being Muslim provided their followers with meaning and moral direction, a sense of purpose and collective identity. But the emergence of so many contrasting and ultimately competing religious projects also led to unintended consequences, the scale of which was magnified by the entanglements of a globalized world. By incorporating the incremental multiplication of so many new versions of Islam, and the central role played by globalization, the big picture presented here helps us understand how global Islam took shape through the confluence of competing forces and conjunctural circumstances across our planet as a whole.

Because this is not a work of theology, it cannot identify a "true" version of Islam and should not be viewed as promoting some versions of Islam as more "authentic" than others. Instead, by adopting the methods social scientists use to study different religions, the approach taken here is to present Islam as what Muslims say it is. Since the wide array of religious activists, organizations, and states have markedly different definitions of Islam, this approach necessarily means accepting for the purposes of discussion that there exists a plurality of different versions of the religion, without advocating for any one of them.

Despite not being a "religious" book, this volume is written to help both Muslim and non-Muslim readers recognize the various organizations competing to claim the authenticity and authority of teaching the "true" version of Islam. The fact remains, however, that there are not only many versions of Islam being promoted around the planet, but also many more of them than previously. Globalization has a lot to do with this state of affairs.

A historical approach allows us to see how Islam has been repeatedly reinterpreted across a century and a half of globalization as increasing numbers of Muslims have claimed the authority to redefine their religion. These modern redefinitions of religion—and the new religious authorities who made them—are central to the emergence of global Islam, which has involved dramatic doctrinal changes. Tracing such transformations enables us to recognize the newness of various versions of global Islam, along with their divergence from traditional ways of being Muslim.

More than merely showing change, a historical approach also explains it by revealing the factors that led particular people in particular places to construct these new versions of Islam, along with the mechanisms they used to export them across borders of various kinds. These mechanisms, which include new forms of mobility, communication, organization, and finance, as well as globally circulating ideas and ideologies of varied provenance, make up the "toolkit" of globalization.

Global Islam is, then, the outcome of a historical process: the interplay between religion and globalization. To understand this process means examining the mechanisms of movement and communication that enabled some religious actors to propagate their version of Islam more widely than others. Yet "widely" should not be taken to mean "everywhere." Because, as we will see, competing versions of global Islam moved through a series of changing geographical coordinates as different regions of the planet were opened and closed to the forces of globalization. These spatial parameters are still in flux today.

Although by the late twentieth century different promoters of global Islam did eventually reach out *to* all regions of the world, they did not emerge *from* those different regions in equal measure. In fact, a remarkably small set of places—especially Egypt, Arabia, and India–Pakistan—have provided a disproportionately large number of global Islamic activists and organizations. This reinforces the point that global Islam cannot be simplistically taken to mean "what all Muslims believe." Rather, the history of global Islam is a story of how the few have tried to change the beliefs of the many.

Even so, during the modern era, many of the world's nominal Muslims have chosen to follow secular rather than religious ideologies. It is therefore important to recognize from the outset that global Islamic organizations do not represent the faith, still less the politics, of all of the world's Muslims. Nonetheless, since this is a study of religious globalization, the following pages cannot dwell on the cultural and nonreligious aspects of Muslim identities, whether individual or collective, even though these are always present and sometimes in conflict with global Islamic models of identity.

Drawing together many detailed studies of the participants, events, and doctrines involved in the making of global Islam, the following chapters show how globalization enabled so many new versions of Islam to be created and then exported around the world. Encompassing India and China, Africa, and the Americas along with the Middle East and Europe, this book provides a pocket-sized map of Islam that is nevertheless of global proportions.

Chapter 1
What is "global Islam"?

A question of definition

In recent years, global Islam has become a pervasive yet opaque subject of contemporary discourse. Both Muslims and non-Muslims struggle to reconcile rhetoric about the unity of Islam with the evident diversity of different forms of the faith that exist around the planet, often in the same city. This book aims to bring clarity to the subject by defining the distinctive characteristics of "global Islam" and showing how its varied manifestations diverged from other, historically prior or geographically localized ways of being Muslim.

As used here, the term global Islam refers to the multiple versions of Islam propagated across geographical, political, and ethnolinguistic boundaries by religious activists, organizations, and states in the age of modern globalization. To speak of global Islam, then, is not to make sweeping statements about Muslims in general. It is to adopt an analytical category that describes the particular forms of Islam promoted by religious actors who have operated across borders by means of the communicational possibilities of modern globalization. To study global Islam is therefore to scrutinize both the common techniques and the competing theologies of different kinds of transnational religious actors, ranging from self-funded solo missionaries to state-funded international organizations.

Bringing together the terms "global" and "Islam" allows us to focus not only on the doctrinal profile of different actors, but equally on their methods of movement and propagation. This is what makes the doctrines promoted by particular activists, organizations, and states not only Islamic but also global. The same approach could be taken to study global Christianity, for example, by comparing the methods of European Protestant missions to the Pacific and the success of African Pentecostal churches in Britain.

Given the global scale of inquiry, using an abstract definition of religion as simply a matter of belief risks vague generalizations that are not only confusing but also misleading. For this reason, the combined focus here is on specific people, their methods of organization and outreach, and the distinct teachings they promote in particular places. This broadly sociological approach has the advantage of avoiding abstract (or "essentialist") models of Islam that depict all Muslims (or all forms of Islam) as fundamentally alike, when the social reality is that they are not.

Moreover, looking at methods of organization, communication, and mobility helps explain why some Muslim religious organizations (and their distinct theologies) have increased their transnational impact by making use of globalization's opportunities while others have not. What characterizes global Islam is therefore not a specific theology, still less a single political vision. Rather, it is methods and scale of outreach: that is, the ability of particular religious actors to propagate their teachings and replicate their organizations and behaviors across boundaries of different kinds.

Yet the history of global Islam is not only a story of diversity. It is also a story of divergence from earlier forms of Muslim religiosity. In order to recognize this divergence, it is helpful to make a categorical distinction between global Islam and world Islam. To recap, as used here, the term global Islam refers to the versions of Islam propagated across geographical, political, and ethnolinguistic boundaries by Muslim religious activists, organizations, and states that emerged in the era of modern globalization. By contrast, the term world Islam refers to the older versions of Islam that developed and adapted to different local and regional environments during the millennium before the onset of modern globalization.

Thinking in terms of world Islam rather than through the older category of "local Islam" (or such regional counterparts as "Indian Islam" or African "*Islam noire*") allows us to acknowledge the interconnections made by premodern Muslim mystics and lawmakers who crossed continents by foot, animal transport, and sailing boats while nonetheless recognizing that theirs was not yet a world (or a religion) that was transformed by the forces of modern globalization.

Far from being identical, global and world Islam have often been in conflict. Many global Islamic organizations have deliberately distinguished themselves from the traditional versions of Islam they seek to replace. As a result, the doctrinal, organizational, and economic foundations of global Islam have evolved in deliberate distinction from the various regional expressions of world Islam. This is in part because the traditional institutions and leaderships of world Islam comprised the time-honored local religious establishments with which the new transnational proponents of global Islam sought to compete.

Thus, over the past century and a half, many promoters of global Islam have seen it as their duty to eradicate the "corrupted" and "erroneous" teachings of world Islam, which often emphasize the powers of Muslim holy men and saintly shrines to work miracles and intercede with God. Consequently, world Islam has survived

1. From the Middle East through Asia and Africa, thousands of shrines around the tombs of Sufi masters were prominent features of world Islam. Larger shrine complexes included mosques, schools, and hostels, such as that of Ahmad Yasawi (d. 1166?) in Kazakhstan.

most fully in regions away from the urban networks through which global Islam has mainly moved.

Because hundreds of millions of Muslims still follow their traditional regional versions of world Islam, global Islam should not be conceived as the sum total of all versions of Islam practiced worldwide. Nor should global Islam be conceived as a single form of religiosity that dominates every region of the globe equally, because not all regions of the planet have been equally impacted by—indeed, open to—the sundry promoters of global Islam.

This approach helps dispel the widespread misconception that global Islam is a homogeneous phenomenon, or indeed that globalization promotes cultural and religious homogenization. In organizational terms at least, the evidence we will examine suggests

9

otherwise, as the opportunities of globalization have enabled an increasing number of religious actors to promote not only different versions of Islam, but rival claimants to religious authority.

For this reason, this book does not use the term "Islamism" that many media and academic commentators have adopted to refer to political versions of Islam. To draw such a clear distinction between "Islam" and "Islamism" obscures the strategy by which promoters of political versions of Islam seek followers by claiming that their teachings are actually normative Islam—indeed, that they are the sole true expression of the faith. Having been coined by French political scientists in the 1980s, the term "Islamism" is not used by such promoters of political Islam themselves, who present their doctrines as either as "Islam" pure and simple, or else as *al-haraka al-Islamiyya* (the Islamic movement). To discuss political Islam as a separate category of "Islamism" therefore obscures the competing claims for authenticity, and the shared use of the same core terms and symbols, that have been so central a feature of Islam's globalization.

To keep a clear grip on these various versions of Islam, this book focuses on the specific people and organizations that promote them. This focus is important because the generic and nonspecific language often used to discuss Islam by both Muslims and non-Muslims obscures the key roles of transnational organizations in defining Islam worldwide. Many such organizations choose not to highlight their names or backgrounds, claiming instead to simply teach an undifferentiated and standard Islam, which makes their history and activities—in fact, their very existence— even harder to recognize.

This is not due to some kind of conspiracy, but rather to the more limited development of denominationalist thinking in Islam as compared with Christianity, which has a long history of speaking of different denominations, whether Catholic, Baptist, Methodist, or Mormon. Yet without identifying Islamic religious organizations and following their trajectories of expansion, it is impossible to understand how different groups of Muslims have come to adopt their specific theological and sometimes political positions. Moreover, attention to the propagational techniques used by transnational religious activists and organizations helps us understand how they have persuaded many Muslims to abandon their former allegiance to world Islam and accept teachings that, despite their rhetoric of antiquity and authenticity, are in many cases quite new.

Beginning around 1870, the modern era of globalization not only saw new Islamic teachings emerge; it also saw the emergence of new types of teachers, who were empowered by the communicational and financial toolkit of globalization. Since this rise of new claimants to religious authority constitutes Islam's most important religious transformation in modern times, before proceeding any further we must take an overview of these changes in religious leadership.

Accounting for "multiple Islams"

Before the emergence of global Islam in the late nineteenth century, there were two basic routes to religious authority among Muslims who followed what we have called world Islam.

The first was through knowledge of the Quran and Hadith (reports of what the Prophet Muhammad said and did), which in turn lent expertise in decision-making with respect to Sharia (religious law) on the basis of interpreting these core texts. Those who claimed authority on this basis were known as *ulama* (learned clerics) and were traditionally educated in seminaries called *madrasas*. Sunni and Shi'i Muslims followed their own different *ulama*. Some *ulama* were appointed to official positions by Muslim royal dynasties (and later, albeit with more limited legal powers, by colonial governments), lending states a role in defining religious authority.

The second traditional route to religious authority was through becoming a Sufi master (variously called a *shaykh*, *murshid*, or *pir*). Such Sufi masters claimed divine mystical contact with God, whose will they could articulate through inspired teachings and whose grace they could channel through performing miracles. The route to becoming a Sufi master was to found, rise up through, or be appointed leader of one of the numerous Sufi brotherhoods. Known as *tariqas* (paths), these brotherhoods were believed to channel the *baraka* (blessing power) and *ma'rifa* (mystical teachings) of the Prophet Muhammad. The brotherhoods' leadership was often hereditary, creating family dynasties of Sufi masters. While their followers could be Sunni or Shi'i, in practice most were Sunni Muslims.

Since it was perfectly possible to master the scriptures (i.e., to become one of the *ulama*) and lead a Sufi brotherhood (i.e., become a Sufi master), these two traditional forms of religious authority often overlapped in the same person, producing what we can call "Sufi-*ulama*." By the mid-nineteenth century, the majority of Sunni Muslims worldwide were aligned to such Sufi-*ulama*, different groups of whom constituted local religious establishments that guided Muslim communities from West Africa across the Middle East to Southeast Asia. Mecca was home to many such authoritative masters.

There were a few exceptions, such as Iran, where powerful Shi'i *ulama* formed a distinct establishment after they persecuted the Iranian Sufi brotherhoods almost out of existence. But by and large, before the onset of modern globalization we can speak of a general worldwide pattern of local and regional religious establishments comprised of Sufi-*ulama* whose brotherhoods and *madrasas* were broadly successful in controlling and thereby stabilizing access to religious authority.

By contrast, from the late nineteenth century, new religious activists began claiming religious authority without having first risen through a Sufi brotherhood or spent years studying to become one of the *ulama*. Moreover, many of these new religious teachers, and the organizations and states they eventually established, were vocal critics of the traditional *ulama* and Sufis whose leadership they were challenging. The result was an incremental fracturing of religious authority as increasing numbers of would-be religious leaders claimed to understand the "true," "pure," or "original" version of Islam that the Sufis and *ulama* had lost sight of. Although some Sufis and rather more *ulama* fought back, this fracturing of religious authority was particularly prevalent among the Sunnis, who constitute around 85 to 90 percent of the world's Muslims.

From around the 1870s, many of the new religious activists who challenged the old Sufi-*ulama* establishment of world Islam were aided by the communicational, financial, and organizational toolkit of globalization. During the modern era, the institutional and organizational basis for claiming religious authority was transformed from a traditional institutional triumvirate of mosque, *madrasa*, and Sufi brotherhood to a plethora of missionary societies, international congresses, political parties, militia groups, nongovernmental organizations, state bureaucracies, satellite television channels, and virtual movements on the internet.

As the routes to religious authority diversified from the narrower criteria recognized in world Islam, increasing access to globalization's toolkit created a multiplier effect, rendering it ever easier to establish new religious organizations or propagate alternative religious teachings. The global Islam that emerged is therefore not characterized by homogeneity and unity, but by heterogeneity, competition for authority, and, in some cases, conflict.

Notably, many of the new methods of organization, revenue generation, and proselytization adopted by the creators of global

Islam were adopted from non-Muslim models in Europe and America, as were key ideas about science, politics, and even ethics. As a result, global Islam can be seen as a varied set of religious outcomes from the mechanical and semantic exchanges of globalization.

The big picture in overview

The world's Muslims have always been connected in certain ways, but never as deeply, broadly, and quickly as in the age of globalization. Historians typically date this era as beginning around 1870, when the far corners of the world were interconnected by postal services, telegraph lines, newspapers, steamships, and intercontinental railroads, along with the European empires and financial institutions that constructed them.

The period between 1870 and the end of the First World War is often identified as the age of "the first globalization." Partly enabled by European imperialism, its onset was marked by the moment when the entire planet was finally connected by the infrastructural web completed with the 1869 opening of the Suez Canal, which linked the Mediterranean Sea and the Indian Ocean, and the Transcontinental Railroad, which bridged the Pacific and Atlantic Oceans. The 1870s was also the decade when printing reached a critical mass among Muslims, half a century after local rulers in Iran, Egypt, and India founded the earliest Muslim-directed printing presses. Together with access to steam travel, printing was the first of a series of technological and communicational mechanisms that made Islamic religious globalization possible. These technologies were to enable new religious activists (and, eventually, organizations) from outside the old establishments of world Islam to gain more followers and broader influence by distributing their claims of religious authority to larger, and more distant, populations than had previously been possible.

The globalization that spread these new networks of steam and print was underpinned by European colonization. As European rule expanded across Asia and Africa, the collapse of Muslim-controlled states and empires aided the emergence of global Islam in two additional ways: first, by weakening the old religious establishments and institutions tied to those precolonial states, and second, by creating anxieties that colonization had occurred because Muslims had strayed from the pure and true version of Islam that new, antiestablishment activists claimed to teach.

Thus, the era of global Islam coincided with the era of Islam's ongoing reformation. The various proponents of this reformation have sought to dissuade Muslims from following the "corrupted" old ways of world Islam, particular those connected with Sufis, who claimed religious authority through a direct mystical relationship with God. However, like the earlier Christian reformation in Europe, this Islamic reformation has been contested and at times bloody, with various individuals, organizations, and states vying to promote their rival reinterpretations.

In response to this reformation, some Sufi-*ulama* from the traditional religious establishment pursued a counter reformation by similarly adopting new forms of proselytizing outreach to defend their versions of Islam. They also amended their doctrines as concessions to their reformist critics. Nonetheless, as we will see, most of the proponents of global Islam were new activists and organizations that emerged from outside the old establishments of world Islam.

The critics of traditional world Islam were not only Muslims: they were also Christian missionaries who spread extensively across Muslim-majority regions opened by colonization. Through their ventures in vernacular printing, organized preaching, and the provision of education and welfare, Christian missionaries presented Muslim religious leaders not merely with competition but with new models of organization and fundraising. In the early twentieth century, the first Muslim missionary organizations began to be formed along the lines of these Christian models, a development that marked a new stage in the organizational evolution of global Islam.

As Europe's empires disintegrated after the Second World War and the nationalist and socialist postcolonial states that succeeded them lost credibility, some of these new organizations formulated political theologies in which Islam provided the answer to political and economic as well as ethical and spiritual dilemmas. In a variety of contexts, sometimes peaceful, sometimes violent, the result was the emergence of different versions of an Islamic state. As a result, modern states such as the Kingdom of Saudi Arabia, the Islamic Republics of Pakistan and Iran, and the Islamic Emirate of Afghanistan used their foreign policies to become a new type of cross-border religious actor.

The half century since 1970 has also seen the emergence of migrant Muslim communities in western Europe, the Americas, and Australasia. With very few permanent and practicing Muslim residents before the late nineteenth century, these regions were effectively blank slates in terms of Islamic institutions and organizations. Although migrants of Muslim heritage carried their own private beliefs with them, the new places in which they settled possessed none of the time-honored Muslim religious establishments and authorities found in the older domains of world Islam across Asia and Africa. As a result, promoters of global Islam faced less competition in the West than in older Muslim regions.

The century and a half between 1870 and 2020 can therefore be divided into three periods—and three corresponding chapters—that saw the rise of new kinds of individual activists, then organizations, then states as promoters of varied and ultimately competing versions of global Islam. To trace these developments is to understand how globalization has led to the increasing contestation of religious authority by providing increasing numbers of (especially Sunni) religious actors with access to the communicational, organizational, and financial tools to propagate their proprietary versions of Islam across geographical, ethnolinguistic, and political boundaries. These incremental and cumulative developments were large-scale historical processes shaped by Muslims and non-Muslims. Far from forming a coherent agenda, still less a "Muslim conspiracy," the emergence of global Islam has led to many unintended consequences through religious and political opposition to pressures from colonialists, nationalists, and socialists.

As well as being extremely varied, with political and nonpolitical versions, global Islam is not synonymous with "what all Muslims believe." For this reason, an important caveat is in order in view of the political sensitivity of Muslim migration. This makes it crucial to recognize the distinction between (a) the promoters of global Islam, who comprise religious activists, organizations, or states that operate transnationally; and (b) ordinary migrant Muslims, who have crossed international borders but are not the active personnel of such organizations. While global Islamic organizations have certainly reached out to Muslim immigrant populations as potential followers, the two should not be simplistically conflated. To determine which forms of Islam (if any) are followed by the millions of notionally Muslim migrants and their second- and third-generation descendants in Europe and North America would require a series of large-scale sociological studies that are beyond the scope of a short book such as this. It would also require looking at various nation-based, even nationalist, expressions of Islam that are necessarily beyond the remit of this book's focus on globalized religiousness.

What is discussed here is the emergence of new types of global religious activism as a range of individuals, organizations, and then states promoted their varying theological and sometimes political agendas across multiple borders. If this cacophony of rival versions of Islam seems bewildering, that is because this is precisely the collective character of global Islam. Rather than producing a single unified Islam, globalization has enabled an incrementally increasing range of religious actors to distribute widely divergent programs of how the world's Muslims should conduct their personal, social, and sometimes political lives. What the many contrasting contributors to global Islam have in common is not a standard set of beliefs or practices, but their shared use of the opportunities of globalization.

Tracing how this came about reveals the degree to which Muslim religiosity has been transformed in modern times through the complex interactions of globalization. Because asking where global Islam came from means examining how Islam was itself transformed through its globalizing transfers. As we will now see, over the course of a century and a half, global Islam increasingly diverged from the regional expressions of world Islam that evolved over the slower course of the previous twelve centuries.

Chapter 2
Islam in the age of empire, steam, and print

Between around 1870 and 1920, the Russian, British, French, and Dutch empires achieved their maximum global influence. From West Africa to Southeast Asia, the vast geography of colonized Muslims stretched from southeastern Europe across central Asia as far as Siberia and encircled the Muslim-populated coasts of Africa from Morocco around the southern cape up to Somalia. The only extensive regions to avoid direct colonization were Iran and Afghanistan, though both were invaded at various points. Yet there was one major Muslim-ruled participant in this imperial world system. This was the Ottoman Empire, which until the end of the First World War ruled what is today Turkey, Iraq, Syria, Lebanon, Israel–Palestine, and Saudi Arabia.

This imperial context is important because the emergence of global Islam cannot be understood in isolation from the impact of Europe (and the Ottoman response to it) by way of Europe's combined roles as the center of the main colonial empires and as the producer of the new technologies of steam and print, which closely integrated the distant regions it ruled. Empire and technology were therefore combined in building the enabling infrastructures and political conditions in which global Islam first emerged.

With the exception of the Ottoman printer Ibrahim Müteferrika (1674–1745), Muslims did not take up printing until around 1820, and it took another half century for Muslim publishing activities to reach a critical mass. Beginning in the 1870s, a range of Muslim religious activists began to make use of not only printing but also train and steamship networks both to travel and to distribute their publications by mail. The first post office in Mecca opened in 1870, and Muslim interregional communication became even easier after the 1874 Treaty of Berne established the General Postal Union for worldwide mail deliveries. In the British, Dutch, French, Russian, and Ottoman Empires alike, this confluence of the new global geographies of empire, steam, print, and post enabled port cities such as Istanbul, Bombay, Singapore, Cairo, and Beirut to become the leading Muslim publishing centers. By 1876, according to one count, there were 107 newspapers and periodicals in the Ottoman Empire alone, with the total number of journals published in all Muslim regions reaching over a thousand by 1919.

Another unintended religious consequence of European colonization was the reduction of the role of the state as the adjudicator of religious orthodoxy and thereby as the promoter of a particular version of Islam. Compared to earlier centuries, when Muslim rulers and their affiliates had patronized countless Sufi pilgrimage sites and traditional *madrasa* seminaries, the colonial period witnessed a tremendous reduction in the role of state officials as religious patrons. As non-Muslims, European officials were anyway in no position to adjudicate on the question of which version of Islam should be followed. Moreover, their pressing need to manufacture consent, or at least acquiescence, to colonial rule meant that they recognized the importance of granting their citizens freedom of religion. This created the great paradox of Muslim life under the rule of non-Muslim empires: political constraint but religious freedom (unless a particular religious figure was regarded as promoting sedition).

The production of new religious ideas increasingly took place in cities that were not under Muslim political jurisdiction, such as Bombay and Singapore, or even London and Paris, and where the state played no role in defining Islam. As Muslim printers expanded their activities in interconnected urban hubs under European rule, the imperial geography of Islamic publishing bore unintended consequences, because access to steam and print technologies allowed new "religious entrepreneurs" to publicize their ideas to larger and more widespread audiences. Inadvertently, European colonization created a fertile environment for a variety of new religious actors to cultivate versions of Islam that often differed considerably from those promoted by the older religious establishments.

The Ottoman campaign for Islamic Unity

While the expansion of European colonial rule meant that for most Muslim regions the state did not serve as a sponsor of global Islam, during the half century before 1920 there was one major exception. This was the Ottoman Empire, for whose leaders Islam became a means of increasing Ottoman influence across a world dominated by Europe.

Beginning around 1870, Ottoman state officials began to promote a policy and broader set of ideas that they labeled *ittihad-i Islam* (Islamic Unity). The broad goal was to unite Muslims worldwide in opposition to the further advance of European imperialism while presenting the Ottoman sultan as the protector of Muslims everywhere. Since the Ottoman motivations were primarily political, the theological requirements (indeed, obstacles) of such unification were regarded as of secondary importance.

The campaign for Islamic unity had two sets of promoters: first, a group of activist intellectuals known as the Yeni Osmanlılar (New Ottomans), who were influential in Ottoman politics between 1860 and 1876; and second, the official circles around Sultan Abd al-Hamid II, who ruled from 1876 to 1909 and revived the ancient title of *khalifa* (caliph or successor to the Prophet Muhammad) as part of the campaign.

Formally organized in 1867 while in exile in Paris, the New Ottomans hoped to revive Ottoman power by adopting European models of government while at the same time reviving the empire's Islamic identity. Yet their ideas were in large part drawn from Europe, particularly science, which they regarded as essential for the revival of Islam. By the early 1870s the New Ottomans were deploying the term *ittihad-i Islam* (Islamic unity) in newspapers and journals they founded, such as *Hürriyet* (Freedom), *Ulum* (Science), *Inkilab* (Revolution), and *Ibret* (Warning). Owing to Ottoman state restrictions on press freedom, many of these publications were printed in European cities such as London, Geneva, Paris, Lyon, and Marseilles. Consequently, the concept of Islamic unity took shape through exposure to various non-Muslim ideologies, such as pan-Hellenism, pan-Slavism, and pan-Orthodoxy, which sought to unite separate populations by appealing to a common identity. Soon a new generation of Arab activists translated the term *ittihad-i Islam* into Arabic as *wahdat al-Islamiyya*. Their publications spread the idea still more widely.

In 1877–78 the Russo-Turkish War provoked the Ottoman state into promoting the campaign, seizing its reins from the New Ottoman activists who first launched it. Key to this cooption was the sultan's titular status as caliph, the notional religiopolitical office as *khalifa* (deputy, or caliph) of the Prophet Muhammad. Subsequently, Sultan Abd al-Hamid II reasserted his status as caliph in an attempt to marshal the growing call for Muslim unity behind the Ottoman Empire as a caliphate to which all Muslims owed loyalty. As the campaign spread to Europe's own empires, the French journalist Gabriel Charmes popularized the term "pan-Islam" to describe the new ideology.

2. Nineteenth-century globalization saw Islam actively promoted in regions with no prior Muslim communities. Conversions were celebrated in the new print media, as with Ottoman newspaper reports on Japan's first Muslim, Shotaro Noda.

For its strategic outreach to Muslim communities beyond the Ottoman Empire, the campaign had to rely on various non-Ottoman cooperators. In 1894 the Iranian Shaykh al-Ra'is (1847–1918) sailed from Istanbul to Bombay to promote the campaign among Iranian and Indian Muslims by publishing in Persian his book *Ittihad-i Islam*. However, the most important non-Ottoman to spread the idea of Muslim solidarity against European power was another Iranian, Jamal al-Din al-Afghani (1838–97). He adopted the sobriquet "the Afghan," which concealed his Iranian Shi'i background, to better promote the cause. Maximizing the possibilities of steam and print for propagating the message of the need for Muslims to unify against their colonizers, al-Afghani traveled widely, publishing numerous works along the imperial infrastructural axis connecting Bombay, Cairo, Istanbul, London, Paris, and St. Petersburg.

With his erstwhile Egyptian follower Muhammad Abduh (1849–1905), al-Afghani published the Arabic newspaper *al-Urwa al-Wuthqa* (The Firmest Link) in Paris. Between 1883 and 1884 its eighteen issues called repeatedly for Muslim global unity in the face of European expansion. As the campaign widened, the languages in which it was promoted through print grew from Turkish and Arabic to Urdu and Persian, as well as the imperial lingua francas of English and French. The journal *Paik-i Islam* (Courier of Islam) appeared bilingually from Istanbul in Urdu and Turkish until British officials persuaded the Ottoman government to halt its publication. Nonetheless, between 1878 and 1908, one Ottoman official, Abu al-Huda al-Sayyadi (1850–1909), published no fewer than 212 books and pamphlets on Islamic unity.

The Ottomans also drew on their diplomatic infrastructure as consulates and ad hoc missions spread the campaign to British India and the Dutch East Indies (now Indonesia), often under the watchful eye of European spies. Emissaries were sent to Zanzibar and the Cape Muslims of South Africa, while in 1913 the Ottoman government sponsored the Palestinian Wajih Zayd al-Kilani

(1883–1916) to sail by steamer to the American colony of the Philippines.

In such ways, the Ottoman campaign for Islamic unity depended on mobile activists, imperial infrastructures, and the printed word. But while successful in spreading the *idea* of Islamic unity, in the absence of a coordinating organizational infrastructure in the various regions where the idea spread, its Ottoman promoters were far less effective in determining how the call for unity would be interpreted and, if at all, acted upon. Thus, while many Muslim sympathizers from beyond the Ottoman Empire were invited to Istanbul, there was no trans regional organizational mechanism to control what they would teach or do when they subsequently returned home.

Eventually, new organizations were founded to coordinate the campaign. In 1913 Ottoman-linked Indians founded the Anjuman-i-Khuddam-i-Kaaba (Society of the Servants of the Kaaba). The same year saw the Cemiyet-i Hayriye-i Islamiye (Islamic Benevolent Society) bring together Turks, Indians, and Arabs from North Africa, Egypt, and Yemen to spread the campaign further. Among its founding members was the tireless Lebanese Druze journalist Shakib Arslan (1869–1946), who subsequently settled in the emerging international hub of Geneva.

Before the First World War at least, the Ottoman goal of the campaign was not to confront the European powers, particularly Britain, which was the Ottomans' chief ally against Russia. Rather, it was an attempt to consolidate Ottoman imperial status as a world power with influence beyond its borders. Yet despite the coordinating attempts of the Ottoman state to channel the call for Islamic unity toward such conservative strategic ends, when its ideas were taken up by independently run organizations and by newspapers and activists who were not controlled by the Ottomans, its political goals and religious orientations became more diffuse, even revolutionary.

As the discourse and vocabulary of Islamic unity spread worldwide, it was appropriated for many different causes, slipping out of Ottoman official control into the hands of revolutionaries who undermined the Ottoman attempt to deploy it to bolster their position among the other, European empires.

One such revolutionary was the Indian Muhammad Barakatullah (1854-1927), who, beginning in the 1880s, traveled from Bombay to reside in the ports of Liverpool, London, New York, Istanbul, Odessa, St. Petersburg, Yokohama, and ultimately San Francisco. In London he cooperated with such nascent organizations as the Anjuman-i Islam (Islamic Society), founded back in 1886 by expatriate Indians to promote Muslim issues in Britain. In Tokyo in 1910 he used the British imperial lingua franca of English to found a journal called *Islamic Fraternity*. Barakatullah subsequently used his global travels to build collaborative relationships with Japanese pan-Asianists, Irish Fenians, and Russian Bolsheviks in pursuit of an anticolonialist program of Muslim reempowerment. After spells in Berlin and Kabul during the First World War, working harder than ever to overthrow the British Empire, he relocated to San Francisco, joining other Indian anticolonialists in printing the Urdu journal *Ghadr* (Rebellion).

The imperial networks of Islamic liberalism

Yet the new spokesmen for Islam who emerged from the British Empire were as often loyalists as revolutionaries, even when responding to the "orientalist" denigration of Islam as benighted and backward. Several itinerant Indian Muslims promoted liberal causes such as the rationality of Islam and its congruence with the findings of science, as well as women's rights and the abolition of slavery, which for the past millennium had been conditionally allowed by the various schools of Islamic law. One of the most prominent Indian Muslims to combine Islamic and British notions of morality and rationality was Syed Ameer Ali (1849-1928). After permanently settling in London in 1904, Ali adapted his training in British common law to rethink the ethical and legal foundations of Islam through the various books and articles he published. By choosing to write in English and residing for decades in London, his ideas spread far and wide across the emerging global Anglosphere.

In addition to his Anglophone Muslim readers in British-ruled India, Burma, East Africa, and Malaya, a newer category of Muslim found Ameer Ali's writings appealing: the British and American convert. One such convert was William Abdullah Quilliam (1856–1932), who opened Britain's first functioning mosque in 1887 in the terraced house where he based his Liverpool Muslim Institute. Another was Muhammad Marmaduke Pickthall (1875–1936), a popular novelist on 'oriental' themes attracted by Ali's Islamic liberalism. Pickthall publicly converted after delivering a paper entitled "Islam and Progress" to the Muslim Literary Society in London's Notting Hill, which was presided over by another liberal Indian lawyer, the Cambridge graduate Abdullah Yusuf Ali (1872–1953). Pickthall subsequently moved to Bombay to become a newspaper editor before relocating to Hyderabad, where he translated the Quran into majestic English that echoed the language of the King James Bible. Meanwhile, Yusuf Ali remained in London, where he became a member of the Liberal Club, and worked on another eloquent English translation, further wrestling access to the scripture from the monopoly held by traditional *ulama* trained in Arabic.

From across the Atlantic, the New York convert Mohammed Alexander Russell Webb (1846–1916) was sailing between Bombay, Rangoon, Alexandria, Istanbul, and Manila. Similarly influenced by the Indian Muslim liberals who wrote in English, after returning to New York, Webb founded the Oriental Publishing Company for his many proselytizing books, as well as his magazine *The Moslem World*, its title a testament to the new religious geography of the period. In 1893 Webb represented Islam at the World Parliament of Religions, a pioneering global conference held in Chicago that was reported in the many new Muslim newspapers.

Even the small community of Tamil-speaking Muslims in British-ruled Sri Lanka was exposed to the new ideas being circulated around the British Empire between London, Cairo, and Singapore. Absorbing new ideas about Islam from both Arabic- and English-language journals, in 1882 the Sri Lankan educational reformer Mukammatu Kasim Cittilevvai (1838–98) founded the newspaper *Muslim Nesan* (Muslim Friend) to promote such liberal causes as women's education and the reconciling of Islam with science. Its articles were read by the Tamil Muslim trading diaspora across India, Sri Lanka, Malaysia, and Burma.

Through its infrastructures, shared language, and political pluralism, the British Empire nurtured a variety of new global propagators of Islam, whose causes ranged from anticolonial revolution to liberal coexistence. They also began to turn English into a global Islamic lingua franca that would enable further blends of religious ideas in turn.

Exporting Islamic reform from Russia

Echoing the intellectual and political interactions of the British Empire, new kinds of religious activists in the Russian Empire also used printing to spread ideas that evolved through their encounters with Europe.

A leading example was Isma'il Gasprinskiy (1851–1914), whose journal *Tercuman* (The Interpreter) called for a rejection of the traditional Islam of his fellow Tatars and its replacement by a rationalized religiousness in which science played a central role. Gasprinskiy and his fellow activists, such as Mahmudkhodja Behbudiy (1875–1919), believed that Russia's Muslims were being held back by the *ulama* and their *madrasa*-based educational system, which had as little room for science as it did for women. The sheer novelty of their approach saw their teachings dubbed "Jadid" (New), in distinction to the "Qadim" (Old) approach of the Sufi-*ulama* establishment, whose authority they rejected.

After a visit to Paris and Vienna, in 1883 Gasprinskiy founded a printing emporium in Russian-ruled Crimea, followed a year later by a school to promote his *usul al-jadid* (new method) of teaching Muslims about science. For his journal *Tercuman* he developed a more accessible form of simplified Turkish that maximized its readership among other Turkic peoples. This act of linguistic outreach was underwritten by the new possibilities of postal subscription, which brought *Tercuman* around 5,000 subscribers (and many more readers) from southeastern Europe to Siberia by way of central Asia. Published alongside his many books, *Tercuman* bore the motto "unity in language, thought and action," which carried echoes of the Ottoman Turkish call for Islamic unity. But Gasprinskiy's emphasis on reinterpreting the Quran and Sharia from rational first principles also echoed what we will see Egyptian reformers promoting at the same time. Print was spreading, blending and fermenting ideas far and fast.

In the early 1900s, Gasprinskiy traveled to the Black Sea coast of Bulgaria and Romania to lecture to the Turkic-speaking Muslims who resided there. In response, several Bulgarian listeners founded their own newspapers, such as *Balkan* (The Balkans) and *Tuna* (The Danube), which passed on his ideas further. In 1908 he even established a short-lived Arabic-language newspaper in Cairo entitled *al-Nahda* (Renaissance). By then the calls for rationalist reform that emanated from the British and Russian empires were becoming intertwined. Even so, it is important to recognize that Gasprinskiy had not founded an organization. Rather, he remained an individual activist making use of the period's communications to promote his new version of Islam to replace that of the traditional Sufi-*ulama*.

3. Raised in Russian-ruled Siberia, Abd al-Rashid Ibrahimov used imperial globalization to promote Muslim unity from St. Petersburg to Tokyo, Bombay, Mecca, and Istanbul.

However, as in the British Empire, other Tatar imperial citizens regarded Russian rule as exploitative and oppressive. One of them was Abd al-Rashid Ibrahimov (1857–1944). Despite being born in the remote Siberian town of Tara, Ibrahimov traveled widely and established two periodicals, *Ülfet* (Reconciliation) and *Najat*

(Salvation), in St. Petersburg. Critical of Russia's treatment of its Muslims, they were banned by the Russian authorities. Persecution led him to exile in the Ottoman capital of Istanbul, where by the 1890s he came under the influence of the impresario of Islamic unity, al-Afghani.

Taking up the call for Islamic unity, Ibrahimov next traveled via the Trans-Siberian Railway and steamship to Japan, which in 1905 had defeated Russia at war. The Ottoman outreach to Japan had already led a journalist called Shotaro Noda (1868–1904) to become the first Japanese Muslim back in 1891, an event widely publicized in the Ottoman press. Now Ibrahimov continued this proselytizing push toward Tokyo by attempting to convert Japanese officials. In 1909 he helped another convert called Mitsutaro "Omar" Yamaoka become the first Japanese to perform the *hajj* (pilgrimage to Mecca). Returning to Istanbul, Ibrahimov published a book about his proselytizing travels. Replete with observations of the colonial oppression of Muslims worldwide, *Alem-i Islam ve Japonyaʿda Intişarı Islamiyet* (The Islamic World and the Spread of Islam in Japan) was one of various printed works from the period that popularized the new geographical category of an "Islamic world."

Like the British Empire, imperial Russia had developed several new types of global Islamic activist as contrasting as Gasprinskiy and Ibrahimov.

The making of Salafism

Meanwhile, in the decades on either side of 1900, two men based in Cairo were laying the basis of a reform movement that would eventually have ramifications worldwide. They were the Egyptian Muhammad Abduh (1849–1905) and his Syrian student Rashid Rida (1865–1935).

The senior of the pair, Abduh, had spent six years in Beirut, Paris, and London, read extensively about Muslims worldwide, and served as editor of Egypt's government newspaper *al-Waqaᶜiᵓ al-Misriyya* (Egyptian Times). Acutely aware of the disunity among Muslims, most vexingly via their many different versions of Islam, early in his career he collaborated with Jamal al-Din al-Afghani's political calls for Islamic unity in response to European power. But after turning away from al-Afghani, Abduh promoted a remedy that was not political but theological. Like Gasprinskiy in Crimea, in Cairo Abduh adopted a simplified prose style in which he wrote many newspaper articles that spread his ideas.

In his *Risala al-Tawhid* (Treatise on Divine Unity), printed in 1897, Abduh propounded a scripturalist but at the same time rationalist version of Islam that used reasoned arguments to make the case for the existence of God and the need for revelation, specifically the Quran. Elsewhere, he rejected what he regarded as both the legal inflexibility of the *ulama* and the corrupting rituals of the Sufis. He also responded to the European criticisms of Muslim "backwardness" by claiming that the Quran was consistent with the findings of modern science. What was holding Muslims back was centuries of unwillingness to rethink the legal requirements and theological doctrines of Islam by means of a rationalist reading of the Quran. Distributed by mail and steamship, his treatise was widely read and translated. Even in the landlocked heart of Eurasia, a Turkic edition appeared in 1911 from one of the Tatar presses of Russian-ruled Kazan, followed by a Chinese translation two decades later.

Abduh's ideas were subsequently taken up and then transformed by his student Rashid Rida. In 1897 Rida, who grew up in Ottoman Syria, moved to Egypt after reading back copies of Abduh and al-Afghani's journal, *al-Urwa al-Wuthqa*. Having turned down the editorship of several journals in Beirut owing to the constraints of Ottoman censorship, in 1898 Rida founded his own journal, *al-Manar* (The Lighthouse), in British-ruled Cairo.

From there the journal's postal subscription model gained it a truly global readership: its subscription base stretched across Russia, Tunisia, India, Sudan, Brazil, Borneo, Thailand, Sierra Leone, Bosnia, China, Malaysia, the Dutch East Indies, Europe, and North and South America. The one region *al-Manar* did not reach from Cairo was the neighboring Ottoman Empire (including Rida's Syrian homeland), where it was banned by Ottoman censors. Mailed worldwide to so many non native readers of Arabic, like Gasprinskiy's Turkic journal *Tercuman*, Rida's *al-Manar* developed a more simplified journalistic style for communicating religious ideas.

The journal made Rida an international religious authority, despite the fact that he never held any formal religious position. Muslims from places as distant as Borneo and Canada (where small numbers had emigrated) mailed him questions, to which he would publish a Sharia-based ruling, or *fatwa*, in reply. Many of these *fatwas* related to the permissibility of using modern technologies, which Rida was generally keen to allow in the cause of modernizing Muslim empowerment. During his decades as editor, he issued over a thousand such *fatwas*. He also occasionally made personal use of imperial travel networks, as in his 1912 steamship and train tour of British India. As a result, Sayyid Abd al-Haq al-Aᶜzami (1873–1924), an Iraqi who taught Arabic at the prestigious Mohammadan Anglo-Oriental College at Aligarh, began translating his ideas into Urdu.

Rida continued to edit *al-Manar* until his death in 1935. He used his journal to promote, develop, then substantially depart from the reformist version of Islam conceived by his mentor, Abduh. Like many other Muslim religious activists in Europe's imperial heyday, Abduh and Rida were preoccupied with the relative weakness of Muslim societies, not least the Ottoman Empire, which they were watching crumble around them. Following Abduh, Rida diagnosed Muslim weakness as the result of their poor command of the new sciences and related technical disciplines that Europeans had mastered, so he encouraged his readers to embrace the findings of science and to rationalize their faith accordingly. Yet to make Islam fit with modern science required jettisoning older forms of religiousness. For Rida, this increasingly meant purging Islam of the rituals and other "superstitions" of the Sufis (especially their belief in miracles). But it also involved a rejection of the practice of *taqlid* (acceptance), by which *ulama* followed the Sharia rulings of medieval predecessors. In practice, this meant rejecting the two main groups of religious authorities: the Sufis and the *ulama*.

What remained of Islam was the Quran, the *sunna* (model) of the Prophet, the behavior of the first few generations of Muslims (called the *salaf*, or ancestors), and Sharia, with the latter subjected to new forms of *ijtihad* (interpretation) to reconcile it with the modern world. By around 1920, this new form of Islam was being called "Salafi" (Ancestralist) for its emphasis on the Quran and the practice of the early Muslims of the first century or so after the Prophet.

Al-Manar served as a global medium for promoting the centrality of Sharia not only to the private piety of individual Muslims (Rida considered Sharia sufficiently comprehensive that its rulings should apply to every element of a believer's life), but also to restoring the collective strength of Islam (which Rida saw as requiring greater legal uniformity and standardization across Muslim societies). Here Rida departed from Abduh in his approach to European rule. Abduh pragmatically saw it as potentially beneficial to Muslims, but Rida instead called for Muslims to unify around a common caliphal leader, a shared Sharia-based legal system, and a stripped-down "ancestral" model of piety.

Ironically, this was ultimately divisive, since it required those who followed the guidance of Rida's legal "lighthouse" to denounce the traditional religious leaders of their home regions. The global Islam of *al-Manar* was therefore in tension with the various versions of world Islam practiced by ordinary Muslims in the regions where it was read by the learned but influential few.

Those few who read *al-Manar* in Arabic furthered its message by founding such Malay-language journals as *al-Imam* (The Leader) in Singapore in 1906 and *al-Munir* (Shining Light) in Padang, West Sumatra, in 1911. They were followed by Calcutta's Urdu *al-Hilal* (Crescent Moon) in 1912, the Mandarin *Tianfang Xueli Yuekam* (Arabic Theology Monthly) of Guangdong (Canton) in 1928, and Mombasa's Swahili *Uwongozi* (Guidance) in 1930. Published in port cities, these journals passed on Rida's ideas, and *fatwas*, to regional audiences, spreading Salafi ideas still further.

In 1912, Rida founded his Madrasa al-Da'wa wa al-Irshad (School of Propagation and Rightful Guidance), effectively a Salafi missionary college. By the time it closed after the First World War, it had a small alumni base drawn from India, Malaysia, and Arabia, as well as Egypt. Despite Rida's failure to establish an enduring Muslim missionary college, he remained fully aware of the importance of efficient religious organization. As early as 1900 he had devoted a series of articles in *al-Manar* to scrutinizing the strategies of Christian and Baha'i missionaries and encouraging Muslims to formally develop their own *tariq al-da'wa* (method of proselytization). But as we will see, it would not be until the late 1920s that such an organization was founded in Egypt to promote his Salafi reform of Islam. Instead, Rida's influence came from thirty-five years spent editing *al-Manar*, the medium that made him the world's first truly global *mufti*, or legal opinion maker.

It is testament to the power of the new communication technologies that Rida gained the religious authority to guide readers from every corner of the globe without ever holding a formal religious appointment.

Itinerant Sufis of the Indian Ocean

Despite the fierce criticism of the rising rationalist and Salafi reformers, some of the Sufi *shaykhs* who had for centuries provided Muslims with religious leadership also made use of the opportunities of imperial globalization. Starting in the 1870s, their main arena of outreach was the Indian Ocean, which was increasingly interconnected by the steamer ports of Aden, Mombasa, Zanzibar, Bombay (now Mumbai), Batavia (now Jakarta), Rangoon (now Yangon), and Singapore.

Many of these steam-powered Sufis were members of the Ba Alawi brotherhood, which originated along the Hadramawt coast of Yemen. From there, Ba Alawi *shaykhs* followed Arab trading routes as far as British-ruled Sri Lanka, Singapore, and the Dutch East Indies (now Indonesia). While many Sufis were nonpolitical—the various empires generally supported the status quo of the Sufi-*ulama* establishment—others voiced their opposition to colonial rule. One such Ba Alawi rebel was Sayyid Fadl bin Alawi (1824–1900), whose resistance to British control of the Indian coast of Malabar led to his being deported after moving there, only to gain more followers during the decades of exile he spent in Mecca, Dhofar, and Istanbul.

By contrast, the East African Sufi Ahmad ibn Sumayt (1861–1925) chose to work for the British. Born in the Comoro Islands into a family of Yemeni merchants affiliated with the Ba Alawi brotherhood, Ibn Sumayt traveled widely after his home islands, annexed by France in 1886, became service stations for oceangoing steamers. He spent the years 1885 to 1888 shuttling between Zanzibar, Istanbul, Cairo, Mecca, and Java before settling in British-ruled Zanzibar, where he was appointed to the official role of *qadi* (judge). He held office there till 1925.

Ibn Sumayt was only one of several Sufi-*ulama* who imported to East Africa a more Sharia-observant and Arabic-based version of

Sufi Islam, one based on his exposure to religious developments in Mecca and Cairo. As British and German conquests connected East Africa's coast more closely with the interior, building the region's first railways, other *shaykhs* followed colonial Swahili soldiers and merchants inland to convert various African peoples to Sufi Islam in Kenya and Tanganyika (now Tanzania).

The early twentieth century also saw the earliest promoters of Sufi Islam reach Europe and America. After emigrating to British-ruled Cairo in 1895, the Swedish painter Ivan Aguéli (Abd al-Hadi Aqili, 1869–1917) converted, then studied briefly at the great medieval *madrasa*, al-Azhar. Subsequently, he rotated between Cairo and Paris, promoting among fellow bohemians his own Europeanized version of Sufism as a means of bridging the cultures of the "East and West."

A few years later, the Indian Sufi Inayat Khan (1882–1927) pursued a parallel path. Originally a musician, after emigrating from Bombay to London he adopted the language of empire to publish *A Sufi Message of Spiritual Liberty* and establish *The Sufi Quarterly* in 1915. In cultured drawing rooms throughout London, Paris, Amsterdam, Lausanne, and San Francisco, Inayat Khan diluted the Islamic legal dimensions of Sufism to formulate a universal spirituality that appealed to his non-Muslim audiences. After he died, several of his Western disciples founded breakaway Sufi circles of their own, which further downplayed the Islamic foundations of Sufism.

However, while some Sufi masters did print their teachings, they were far less effective in promoting and distributing them. There was certainly no Sufi equivalent to the widely distributed rationalist, Salafi, and otherwise anti-Sufi journals being founded in the late nineteenth century, even in the Sufis' key catchment area of the Indian Ocean. When Zanzibar's first Arabic newspaper, *al-Najah* (Success), was established in 1911, it was modeled on the reformist journals of Cairo, such as *al-Manar*, that sought to undermine Sufi Islam. As early as the 1900s, outside the salons of Paris and San Francisco, the Sufis were making less of the opportunities of globalization than their ascendant rivals.

Globalizing Shi'ism

However, the period between 1870 and 1920 saw effective new forms of outreach by traditional Shi'i religious leaders, who not only expanded but centralized their authority. This set in motion what would become a distinct trajectory of Shi'i globalization that diverged from the fragmentation of religious authority among Sunni Muslims.

Empire again played a key enabling role. After the titular head of the minority Ismaili Shi'is, Aga Khan I (1804–81), moved from inland Iran to British-ruled Bombay in 1846, he and his son Aga Khan II (1830–85) reconnected the scattered Ismaili communities around them as the living imam descended from Muhammad. Via roving emissaries, printed texts, and the canny use of colonial law, the Aga Khans established their authority over the Ismaili diaspora in India, Iran, and East Africa in a manner that had been impossible during the previous centuries they had spent residing in the remote interior of Iran.

Turning to the majority Twelver Shi'is, cheaper steam travel across the Indian Ocean enabled larger numbers of Shi'i pilgrims to visit the Iraqi holy cities of Karbala and Najaf. Many came from colonial India, which possessed a large Shi'i minority whose gifts channeled further revenues to the Shi'i *ulama* of Iraq, as did the Oudh Bequest, a huge endowment from an Indian prince overseen by British administrators. As Lebanese Shi'i merchants followed French colonial networks as far as Senegal and Indian Shi'i traders grew rich in British East Africa and Burma, new financial mechanisms aided the *ulama* in collecting religious taxes from them. These revenue streams helped cement the influence of *ulama* based (or trained) in Iraq over ordinary Shi'is in Syria,

Lebanon, Iran, the Persian Gulf, and India. Pious donations enabled Indian Shi'i students to study at Iraqi *madrasas* before returning home to positions of authority based on their continued compliance with the rulings of senior *ulama* in Iraq. The Shi'i *ulama*'s influence also expanded in Iraq itself, as Arab tribes converted to Shi'ism despite Ottoman attempts to prevent it.

Doctrine was equally crucial to the consolidation of the Shi'i *ulama*'s authority. In the second half of the nineteenth century, the influential cleric Murtada al-Ansari (1781–1864) formalized the doctrine that every Shi'i Muslim must follow the rulings of a *marja' al-taqlid* (authority to be followed), necessarily a highly ranked member of the *ulama*. The spread of printing to Iraq allowed treatises on the topic to be published. Mail services rendered the principle a practical reality for ordinary Shi'is who lived far from the base of their *marja'* in Karbala or Najaf but could mail in requests for guidance.

Although the institutionalization of the *marja'* was complex and contested, the result was that Shi'i Islam underwent a centralization of religious authority around a shrinking number of senior *ulama* known as *ayatullahs* (signs of God).

Connecting Southeast Asia and China

Mirroring the influence of migrant Shi'i *ulama* trained in Najaf, the increasing ease of travel around the Indian Ocean enabled Sunni *ulama* who had studied in Mecca and Medina to establish themselves in East Africa, Indonesia, India, and even Thailand.

In some cases, Southeast Asian émigrés such as Muhammad Nawawi al-Bantani (1813–97) and Ahmad Khatib al-Minangkabawi (1860–1916) established themselves in Mecca, where they enabled many students from their home regions to undertake formal studies with them then return home to spread their teachings in towns and villages across Southeast Asia. Taking advantage of communication technologies, as early as 1859 al-Bantani became the first Southeast Asian scholar to send his Arabic writings to Cairo for printing, while in 1885 Ahmad Zayn al-Fatani (1856–1906) began overseeing the printing of religious works in vernacular Malay from Mecca.

As erstwhile students returned to their home regions across the Indonesian archipelago, taking these books with them, these newly minted *ulama* promoted a closer observance of Sharia they had learned in Mecca. Even as they remained members of the Sufi brotherhoods, who had long traversed the ocean on a smaller scale, a new generation of student activists used legal arguments to critique local Sufi establishments and rituals for overstepping the boundaries of religious law. They sought to replace regional forms of world Islam, whose customary rituals were not necessarily in line with the precepts of Sharia, with the more scripturalist and legalist form of religion they had learned in Arabia.

The institutional vehicles for these changes were small-scale seminaries known as *pesantren*, founded as Malay former students returned from Mecca or Medina to settle in small towns and villages across Southeast Asia. Such institutions in turn became feeder schools preparing local students for higher studies in Mecca. During the 1880s and '90s, Abd al-Qadir al-Fatani ran a school in Bendang Daya, where Malay Muslims lived under oppressive Buddhist rule in Thailand.

In the 1870s, small groups of Malay students also began studying at the medieval *madrasa* of al-Azhar in Cairo, where they were exposed to the range of new religious ideas emerging in the Arab Middle East, whether the rationalist reformism of Muhammad Abduh or the Ottoman campaign for unity. In 1912 Malay students at al-Azhar founded a journal aptly entitled *al-Ittihad* (Unity), while the educational reformer Oemar Said Tjokroaminoto (1882–1934) established the Sarekat Islam

4. Members of the first small Salafi circles were assiduous adapters of print media, spreading their message worldwide through the new international postal system. No journal was more influential than Rashid Rida's *al-Manar*.

41

(Islamic Union) in Batavia (now Jakarta) with financial support from Arab and Javanese traders. That same year, the ethnic Minangkabau scholar Hajji Rasul (1879–1945) founded a seminary in Padang Panjang, Sumatra, to disseminate Abduh's ideas more widely. Seven years later, its graduates founded Sumatera Thawalib (Students of Sumatra), one of Southeast Asia's earliest modern religious organizations, to reform the local traditions of world Islam.

By this time, Hui (ethnic Chinese) Muslims were also studying in Mecca. The most important new activist among them was Ma Wanfu (1849–1934), who, after returning to his native region of Gansu in 1888, founded the Yihewani (from the Arabic *al-ikhwan*, "brotherhood") in opposition to China's long-established Sufi brotherhoods. Once Rida's *al-Manar* reached China, the Yihewani began promoting Salafi reformist texts over the older Persian Sufi syllabus that had flourished for centuries among the Hui in China.

In Southeast Asia as in China, the easier connections with the Middle East afforded by steam and print empowered new activists and nascent organizations that sought to undermine the regional forms of Islam that had spent centuries adapting to their local environments.

India's messianic missionaries

So far, we have seen many individual activists, Ottoman-sponsored networks of them, and regional organizations in Southeast Asia, but no interregional religious organizations that reached across borders. But one such organization did emerge in the age of empire, steam, and print. This was the Ahmadiyya, whose successful proselytizing provoked widespread condemnation for what other Muslim authorities considered the heretical character of their messianic beliefs. It was nonetheless the first transnational Muslim missionary organization.

The Ahmadiyya was founded around 1885 in the Indian region of Punjab by Mirza Ghulam Ahmad (1835–1908), who claimed to be both the Messiah and the Mahdi promised by Christian and Islamic eschatology. While this brought him denunciations from rival religious authorities, his claims also won him followers, especially after his decision to adopt the organizational methods of Christian missionaries. Since, like many other Indian Muslims, Mirza Ghulam Ahmad believed in loyalty to the British Empire, it was not only current Muslims who became his followers. In 1913 the Ahmadiyya missionary Khwaja Kamal-ud-Din founded the Woking Muslim Mission at Britain's first purpose-built mosque, outside London. It attracted high-profile British conversions that were publicized worldwide in its journal, *The Islamic Review*.

In 1914, other followers founded the Ahmadiyya Anjuman Isha'at-i Islam (Ahmadiyya Society for the Propagation of Islam) in the Indian (now Pakistani) city of Lahore. Ahmadiyya journals were soon being distributed in Arabic, Persian, Urdu, and English; they included addressed pledge forms that readers could tear out, fold, and mail, in a convenient act of conversion to Ahmadiyya Islam. In effect, the Ahmadiyya had established a Muslim countermission that spread across the entirety of the British Empire as far as Britain, Canada, West Africa, Malaysia, and Australia. In January 1920, another Indian missionary, Mufti Muhammad Sadiq, embarked from London on the SS *Haverford* bound for America. In Philadelphia, then Chicago and Detroit, Sadiq's preaching against racism and his magazine *Muslim Sunrise* laid the foundations of African American Islam.

Although rival Muslim religious authorities rejected the Ahmadiyya, their successful adaptation of the organizational methods of Christian missionaries would subsequently be imitated by the founders of other new Muslim organizations.

Two failed political campaigns

In November 1914, the age of imperial globalization initiated its destructive last act as the Ottomans entered the First World War on the side of the German and Austro-Hungarian empires. Acting in his capacity as caliph, Sultan Mehmed V (r. 1909–18) called on Muslims worldwide to make jihad against the Triple Entente of the British, French, and Russian empires. The call for jihad was translated into Arabic, Urdu, Persian, and Tatar. Promoting the cause, in 1914 the Ottoman Ministry for War launched the journal *Jihan-i Islam* (The Islamic World) in parallel editions in Urdu, Persian, Turkish, and Arabic; in 1916 it was joined by the Istanbul-based Arabic journal *al-'Alam al-Islami* (The Islamic World). But the joint Ottoman–German call for jihad failed to provoke a significant militant response: millions of Muslim soldiers fought for the British, French, and Russians.

However, when the Ottomans were defeated in 1918, the decades of Ottoman campaigning for Islamic unity did pay a belated if ultimately futile dividend. Between 1919 and 1924, an international network of Indian Muslim activists sought to pressure the British government into preserving the Ottoman Caliphate. A crucial role was played by the print-based publicity of Muhammad Ali (1878–1931) and Shaukat Ali (1873-1938), brothers and newspaper editors from Delhi, as well as Abu al-Kalam Azad (1888–1958), who ran several pro-Ottoman newspapers in Calcutta that the British closed down in turn. In terms of formal organizational structure, the campaign was conducted through the relatively small and poorly financed All-India Central Khilafat Committee, formed in November 1919 at a conference called to promote the cause. It sent emissaries to Istanbul, Jeddah, and London, where they founded the Islamic Information Bureau, which in turn published a series of English-language weeklies calling for global Muslim unity.

When the new secular nationalist rulers of Turkey abolished the office of caliph in 1924, the Khilafat movement collapsed. It left a legacy of campaign experience, common ideas, and networked individuals, but no enduring organizational structure. Moreover, global Islamic activists now faced a double setback: the end of the sole Muslim-ruled empire and the rise in many Muslim regions of secular nationalists and socialists.

Over the previous half century, since 1870, the interconnections of imperial globalization had enabled a variety of Muslim religious activists to create networks of individuals with similar goals. Nonetheless, aside from the Ahmadiyya (regarded by most Muslims as heretics), by the early 1920s there were still no global Islamic organizations that could direct these networked individuals toward common goals. What few organizations that had been formed were ad hoc groupings, with poor funding methods and limited mechanisms for expansion, let alone coordinating mass memberships. But such new and enduring types of organization were about to emerge, albeit in a period of ascendant and sometimes aggressive secularization.

Chapter 3
Defending Islam from the secular world order

The fifty years between 1920 and 1970 witnessed the collapse of the empire-based world system in a two-stage process after the First and Second World Wars and its replacement by a more bordered world of secularizing nation-states. Much was inherited from the previous period both by way of an enabling global infrastructure and by way of shared religious concepts, such as the calls for *ittihad* or *wahdat* (Islamic unity), *tajdid* (renewal), and *islah* (reform). But much was also new to the decades after 1920. Original doctrines would also emerge, along with organizations to promote them. Moreover, the collapse of the Ottoman Empire removed Istanbul's role as a focal node of global Islamic aspirations and activities, while the emergence of the Soviet Union saw the brutal rupturing of the Muslim networks that had spread across the Russian Empire.

While some parts of the globe (particularly the vast dominions of the Soviet Union and the People's Republic of China) fell off the map of global Islam, others (particularly cities in western Europe and North America) found a larger place on it. Other regions— continental interiors and rural areas in particular—remained as "off network" during this second period as they had been during the preceding one. Thus, before the 1970s the interior of the African continent remained relatively impervious to the promoters of global Islam, whose more limited outreach to Africa was limited to port cities, their hinterlands, and a few inland hubs. Rather than imagining global Islam as encompassing the entire planet, then, we should recognize both the unevenness of its spread and the very real political barriers it faced between 1920 and 1970.

As empires receded, the rise of secular nationalism in the Middle East, India, and elsewhere in Asia presented a powerful ideological threat to those who promoted Islamic visions of society and politics. Despite what we have seen of the Ottoman-led attempts to promote Islamic Unity as a counter to European power, the most successful anticolonial movements were ultimately those associated with nationalism and socialism. As a result, religious authorities were sidelined by new nationalist and socialist elites across the Middle East, Asia, and Africa, not to mention the Soviet Union and China, whose two-stage turn toward socialism effectively sealed off much of Eurasia to border-crossing Islamic activists.

Broadly speaking, the new secularizing governments were less sympathetic to the demands of Muslim religious authorities than the European empires, which had sought legitimacy through policies of noninterference and occasional promotion of Islamic causes. Whether in monarchist Iran or communist China, religious leaders were regarded by self-styled "progressive" socialists and nationalists as reactionary spreaders of backward superstition. Socialist governments were particularly hostile, closing mosques, demolishing shrines, murdering religious leaders, and severely restricting the *hajj*. Having emerged under the dense shadow of European colonial power, global Islam matured in the era of secular socialism and nationalism as tightly knit cadres of activists gained cohesion through hard decades of protest and sometimes imprisonment. As a result of these historical circumstances, many of the new religious organizations that took shape in this period acquired an oppositional stance to secularism that became embedded in their foundational doctrines.

The nascent global Islamic organizations of the 1920s also faced powerful state-funded rivals. The replacement of empires by nation-states (including the socialist nation-states of the Soviet Union) saw the establishment of state-supported national religious institutions expressly intended to undermine what were regarded as the supranational loyalties of global Islam. In 1924, the new Republic of Turkey established a Diyanet İşleri Başkanlığı (Directorate of Religious Affairs) to replace the transnational ties of the caliphate with an official Islam aligned with Turkish nationalism. After Soviet purges reduced the number of mosques from tens of thousands to just 400, in 1944 four regional Spiritual Directorates were established to control Islamic activity. In 1953, the People's Republic of China followed suit by founding the Zhōngguó Yīsīlánjiào Xiéhuì (Islamic Association of China), which to this day officially administers China's Muslims.

In line with the broader economic policies of nationalism and socialism, many borders were closed to would-be Muslim globetrotters, particularly those around the Soviet Union (from 1922), Eastern Europe (from 1945), and China (from 1949). When border controls were later relaxed, socialist states such as Yugoslavia created official organizations as attempts to coopt Muslim internationalism for their own strategic purposes.

As for Asia, beginning in 1947 an inward-turning independent India played a reduced role in global Islam relative to the status it had had as the geographic and demographic center of the British Empire. Nonetheless, the northern sector of British India (renamed "Pakistan") inherited, then expanded the Muslim networks that had emerged under empire.

The human and cultural input into global Islam changed in response to these geopolitical transformations. Turkish, Soviet, southeastern European, and then Chinese secularization policies meant that, from Bulgaria to Xinjiang, the Turkic contribution to global Islam decreased dramatically. This left two key regions—and their main lingua francas of Arabic and English—as the chief export zones of new religious doctrines and the new organizations that spread them. Those regions were Egypt and Pakistan. It is no coincidence that they were both former British colonies at the center of imperial communication networks and deeply exposed to European ideas, scientific and religious alike. This imperial legacy would shape the subsequent contours of the two key doctrinal orientations that spread from Egypt and India—namely Salafism and Deobandism—whose promoters embraced the communication opportunities made available by empire while rejecting the broader culture of the colonizers.

In the decades after the First World War, promoters of global Islam were further aided by the emergence of two new postcolonial states. These were Saudi Arabia, formally established in 1932 after independence from Ottoman rule, and Pakistan, established in 1947 after independence from Britain. Together they became key bastions of global religious activism amid a new world order dominated by secular nationalists and socialists.

Even so, it was not states that were promoting global Islam in the half-century heyday of socialism and nationalism. In contrast to the previous period of mobile individuals enabled (and in the Ottoman case promoted) by empires, the five decades between 1920 and 1970 were chiefly characterized by the rise of transnational Islamic organizations, including missionary societies and congresses.

A parallel development was the creation of new institutional spaces for Islam around the globe. This effected a reterritorialization of Islam by which mosques were constructed in western Europe and the Americas during the same decades when they were closed in the Soviet Union, China, and southeastern Europe. In 1921, the first purpose-built mosque in the United States was erected in the Detroit suburb of Highland Park; in 1924, the Wilmersdorfer Moschee opened in Berlin; in 1926, the first purpose-built mosques in London and Paris were inaugurated with the Fazl Mosque and Grande Mosquée de Paris; in 1929, Brazil's first mosque, the Mesquita Brasil, was constructed in São Paulo; in 1935, Japan's first mosque opened in the port city of Kobe; and in 1938, Canada's earliest mosque welcomed worshippers in Edmonton.

The Sufi shrines and lodges that were so characteristic of world Islam were notably absent from this institutional expansion to new regions. The spread of Islam to western Europe and the Americas did not witness the building of any Sufi institutions on

5. From late colonial India, the missionary Ahmadiyya spread an appealing message of pacifism and fraternity that won many followers in the interwar period. They founded Germany's first permanent mosque, the Wilmersdorfer Moschee in Berlin.

the scale or with the grandeur of the new mosques. Although individual Sufis continued to cross borders in search of new followers, having already fallen behind their rivals amid the Muslim printing revolution, they would found no transnational institutions or organizations to rival those of their growing number of antagonists.

Exporting Egyptian Salafism

From his base in Cairo, by the 1920s the pioneering Salafi Rashid Rida was distributing his journal *al-Manar* to readers as distant as Buenos Aires and Singapore, promoting a return to the Islam of *al-salaf* (the ancestors). He interpreted the Quran and Hadith anew, without recourse to earlier readings and rulings. By rejecting the centuries of tradition that separated present-day Muslims from the first generations, he hoped his stripped-down religious teachings would enable Islam to integrate the sciences that underwrote the power of Europe. He also hoped that a simplified common creed, swept clean of the regional variations of world Islam, would unify the planet's Muslims in the face first of colonialism and then of nationalism.

This purported "return" to the pure Islam of the ancestors necessitated abandoning the rituals and doctrines of the Sufis, whom Rida regarded as the principal cause of Muslim moral, intellectual, and political decline. Here lay the central irony of Rida's Salafi vision: it could only promote a unified global Islam by condemning the Sufi foundations of world Islam and in so doing increase inter-Muslim conflict. The doctrine of *hisba* (forbidding wrong and commanding good), which would emerge as one of the core Salafi tenets, explicitly encouraged denunciation of non-Salafi (especially Sufi and Shi'i) Muslims.

Starting in the 1920s, Rida's small circle in Cairo used three main mechanisms for expanding their influence beyond Egypt: printing books and journals, undertaking proselytizing tours, and penetrating the emerging bureaucracy of Saudi Arabia. Formed through the break up of the Ottoman Empire, Saudi Arabia presented Rida with the last hope for Islam to defy the threefold onslaught of European colonialism (the empire's other Arab provinces had been mandated to Britain and France), secular nationalism (spreading through Egypt, Turkey, and Iran), and godless socialism (which Bolshevists were busily promoting among Muslims). Since affordable steam travel had greatly increased the numbers of Muslims making the *hajj* from every corner of the world—the 1920s even saw the arrival in Mecca of converts from Japan—the Saudi conquest of the holy city in 1924 offered Rida's small cadre of Salafis a unique opportunity.

Between 1926 and 1928, Rida dispatched to Mecca and Medina at least eight of his closest disciples, including two graduates of his short-lived missionary school. One of them, Muhammad Hamid al-Fiqi (1892–1959), was appointed president of the newly formed Meccan Department of Printing and Publication, which he used to found the first Saudi journal, *al-Islah* (Reform). In 1927, a branch of Cairo's original Salafiyya Press was opened in Mecca. The following year, two more of Rida's acolytes—Muhammad Abd al-Razzaq Hamza (1890–1972) and Taqi al-Din al-Hilali (1893–1987)—were placed in charge of educating the *mutawwif* (guides) that all pilgrims were now required to employ. As Salafi doctrines were integrated into the pilgrimage and Sufi *bid'at* (innovations) deleted from it, the *hajj* was deployed to distribute Salafism back to the pilgrims' homelands. Between the 1930s and 1950s, the construction of other Saudi state institutions cemented Salafism into the emerging religious bureaucracy and educational system. This in turn promoted Salafi ideas via the workers and students who came to Saudi Arabia from other regions of the world.

Yet for all their antipathy to European primacy, Rida's acolytes were highly educated products of the cosmopolitan colonial capital that was Cairo. At first, they hoped to restrain the more extreme and antiscientific tendencies of Saudi Arabia's provincial and often poorly educated Wahhabi *ulama*, whose *taqlid* (adherence) to the teachings of Muhammad ibn Abd al-Wahhab (d. 1792) they rejected alongside adherence to other authorities after the first centuries of the pious "ancestors." But over time, Rida's émigré Salafi emissaries were forced to compromise with their Saudi hosts by abandoning the rationalist and ecumenical aspirations of Abduh and Rida and adopting the more puritanical and sectarian views of the Wahhabi *ulama* affiliated with the Saudi royals. While Rida's Salafi ambassadors failed to moderate the Wahhabis, they rehabilitated their poor reputation by presenting them as more respectable followers of a Salafi *manhaj* (method) supposedly based on the practices of the original ancestral Muslims. Subsequently, the compound Salafi-Wahhabism exported from Saudi Arabia would be more rigid and sectarian than the modernizing and moderate Salafism developed earlier in Egypt.

Yet, however important Saudi Arabia would subsequently become in the global promotion of this "Wahhabized" version of Salafism, it was only one of the routes through which Rida's ideas expanded their influence. The global reach of Rida's journal *al-Manar* attracted to Cairo a series of student migrations that were amplified by the fact that the city was also home to al-Azhar, the most prestigious medieval seminary to survive into modern times.

A case in point is the small but influential cadre of Hui (ethnic Chinese) Muslims sent to al-Azhar during the 1920s and '30s. One of them, Muhammad Ma Jian (1906–78), collaborated with Rida on Chinese translations of several works by Rida's own teacher, Abduh. Several other Hui students were associated with Muhib al-Din al-Khatib (1886–1969), the Syrian founder of Cairo's original Matba'a al-Salafiyya (Salafi Publishing House). On returning to China, they became highly influential in the Chinese Salafi Yihewani movement, steering many Hui away from the Sufi texts studied in China for centuries and back to the scripture. To this end, in 1945 Ma Jian completed a Chinese translation of the Quran to return his countrymen to the Islam of scripture.

Midway between the Middle East and India, the British-ruled port of Aden in Yemen also became an important Salafi node. In the 1920s and '30s, the Indian, Arab, and African Muslims who sojourned there were exposed to stinging critiques of Sufi practices made by the Nadi al-Islah al-ʾArabi al-Islami (Arab Islamic Reform Club). Further south, *al-Manar* and other products of the Salafi Publishing House reached readers of Arabic in East Africa, where Rida's message of reempowering Muslims through religious reform held great appeal in a region where former Muslim elites had been replaced by British rulers, who had in turn empowered African Christian converts. In 1932, the Swahili notable al-Amin Mazrui (1875–1947) founded another newspaper called *al-Islah* (Reform). Issued in Arabic and Kiswahili, it reached many readers along the East African coast, urging them to renounce the old rituals of world Islam. By now Salafi ideas were spreading throughout the countries of the Indian Ocean, which only a few decades earlier had been a Sufi stronghold.

The case of Rida's Moroccan disciple Taqi al-Din al-Hilali illustrates how the early Salafis reached out to so many regions. Raised in a remote Saharan oasis, al-Hilali left for studies in colonial Algeria before moving to Egypt in 1922. After employment in Saudi Arabia, he taught in Iraq, then in 1930 moved to India to teach Arabic (and learn English) at the influential Nadwat al-Ulama *madrasa* in Lucknow. A generation earlier, its founders had tried to revive the teaching of Arabic as a global Muslim lingua franca after their steamship visits to the Middle East. Through teaching in Lucknow and printing in Bombay, al-Hilali introduced Salafi ideas to many Indians, one of whom founded the Arabic journal *al-Diya* (Illumination), which in circulating as far as North Africa deepened India's contact with Arab Salafis. But al-Hilali's peregrinations were far from over. Next, after several years spent teaching in the Iraqi port of Basra,

Hilali, Muhammad Taqi al-Din

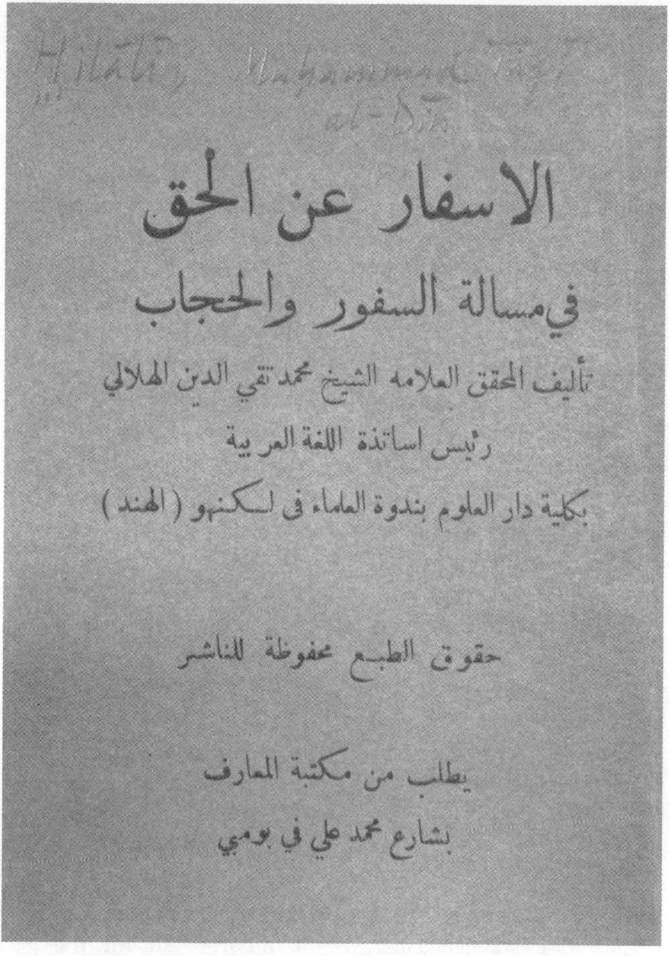

الاسفار عن الحق

في مسالة السفور والحجاب

تأليف المحقق العلامه الشيخ محمد تقي الدين الهلالي

رئيس اساتذة اللغة العربية

بكلية دار العلوم بندوة العلماء فى لكنهو (الهند)

حقوق الطبع محفوظة للناشر

يطلب من مكتبة المعارف

بشارع محمد علي في بومبي

6. From their initial headquarters in Cairo, the small but dedicated cadre of Salafis spread their teachings far and wide. After moving to India, Rida's Moroccan student Hilali printed short treatises in Bombay.

he went to Geneva as the guest of the Lebanese impresario of Islamic unity Shakib Arslan (1869–1946). In 1936, Arslan helped al-Hilali enroll in university in Bonn and then in Berlin, which since the 1920s had become Mitteleuropa's main Muslim hub. Al-Hilali remained in Germany throughout the Second World War, learning the propagational potential of the new medium of radio while making Arabic broadcasts for the Nazis' Radio Berlin. Its broadcasts denounced the evils of British colonialism in the Middle East and Jewish complicity in Palestine, which was partly how Salafi reform became entrenched in politics.

Whether by studying with Rida's other itinerant disciples, such as the West African Muhammad Amin al-Shinqiti (1876–1932), or by reading their many publications, by the end of the Second World War the seeds of Salafism had been transplanted from Egypt to Europe, India, Indonesia, and China. In the postwar decades, Salafi circles were established in all these regions, which sent out their own emissaries in turn.

This Salafi globalism is encapsulated in the writing of *Jawab al-Ifriqi* (Answer of the African) by Abd al-Rahman al-Ifriqi (1908–57). Comprising answers to questions posed by an Indian from Malabar to an African from Mali who lived in Medina, the *Jawab* was published in Cairo in 1946 and from there distributed to Arabic readers worldwide.

Muslim Brothers on the Suez Canal

The spread of Salafism was also aided by a new religious organization established in the Egyptian port of Ismailia in 1928. Its name was al-Jama'at al-Ikhwan al-Muslimin (Society of Muslim Brothers). Better known as the Muslim Brotherhood, its founder was a schoolteacher called Hasan al-Banna (1906–49).

In his youth, al-Banna was an avid reader of Rida's *al-Manar* before becoming directly associated with Rida's circle as a student in Cairo. Then, as a young schoolteacher posted to Ismailia, al-Banna became appalled by what he saw as the collapse of Muslim morality along the cosmopolitan Suez Canal Zone. Amid the high-water mark of Christian missionary activity in Egypt, Ismailia and Port Said were rocked by heated controversies about Swedish missionary conversions of Muslims, particularly orphans and young women. In response, al-Banna helped organize opponents to the missionaries under the banner of protecting Islam.

In 1928, al-Banna founded the first small circle of Muslim Brothers, comprising six men who took a formal oath—a subsequent requirement of joining the Brotherhood—to serve as *jund* (troops) in the service of Islam. He learned to solicit and gather donations and was soon overseeing other branches along the Canal Zone, which arguably constituted the most intensely globalized region of the Middle East. Permanent revenues were subsequently assured by compulsory membership fees, later supplemented by industrial investments and donations from wealthy sympathizers. Soon al-Banna was initiating Islam-oriented social-welfare programs to compete with the schools, orphanages, and hospitals built by foreign Christian charities.

By 1931, the Brotherhood had opened a boys' school called the Islamic Freedom Institute, followed the next year by the School for Mothers and Believers, then by another school called the Muslim Sisters. Each of them trained pupils to undertake *da'wa* (propagation) alongside adult members. Regularly writing for (and eventually editing) *al-Manar*, al-Banna then returned to Cairo, where, through the Salafi Publishing House, he issued his own weekly newspaper, *al-Ikhwan al-Muslimin* (Muslim Brotherhood). This allowed him to refine his message of rendering Islam into a total system whose laws were the final arbiter on every aspect of life, private and public, spiritual and political.

In 1933, the Brotherhood organized the first of what would become its regular annual conferences. These served to centralize control of its growing number of followers around al-Banna's teachings. The first conference was dedicated to combating Christian missionaries. By the second annual conference in 1934, there were already more than thirty branches of the Brotherhood around Egypt. The following year marked a crucial stage in the export of al-Banna's message: his first delegation left Egypt for Palestine, from where they established contacts in Syria and Lebanon.

From its outset, both in terms of the provision of social welfare and professionalized proselytization, the Brotherhood learned to adapt the Christian missionaries' methods. Yet the Brotherhood was dedicated to the cause of what al-Banna conceived as a specifically *da'wa salafiyya* (Salafi proselytization). Although from his rural childhood he remained fond of Sufi devotional practices, overall he considered the Sufi brotherhoods to be a cause of division and backwardness among Muslims. This placed him in line with Rida and the wider Salafi rejection of Sufi authority to return Islam to the teachings of scripture and the early ancestors. But crucially, for al-Banna this ancestral Islam included a Sharia-ruled state of the kind he believed the Prophet Muhammad had founded in Medina.

Although he modeled his politics on this vision of early Medina, al-Banna constructed his ideas in oppositional dialogue with a monolithic "West" that he imagined (having never left Egypt) as the antithesis of his Islamic "East." He believed this godless West (in which he included both capitalist countries and the Soviet Union) was obsessed with dividing and destroying the Muslim-ruled empires of what he looked back on as a medieval golden age. Here he shared other Salafis' concerns with the weakness of Muslims amid the dividing forces of colonialism, socialism and nationalism. But as his thinking developed, he went further than the first generation of Salafis by developing a political theology that offered the collective solution to Muslim political, moral, and cultural decline by founding a new form of state run on Islamic principles. In the words of what would become the Muslim Brotherhood's most famous slogan, "The Quran is our constitution and jihad our path."

As this rallying call suggested, struggle—even violent struggle— was permitted on this path to establishing the Islamic state that would offer Muslims salvation in both this world and the next. By the late 1930s, the Brotherhood had formed a paramilitary band called the *firaq al-jawwala* (Rover Troops) as part of a larger expansion program that saw overall membership grow from 5 branches in 1930 to 500 by 1940. With the Rovers' street fighting and the other Brothers' agitation against the British in Palestine following the outbreak of the Second World War, by 1941 al-Banna was in prison. But by the time he was assassinated by Egyptian secret police eight years later, the Brotherhood had 2,000 branches of perhaps half a million members, both male and female.

Although al-Banna was close to the original circle of Salafis around Rida, there were important differences between them, in terms not only of his innately political conception of Islam but also of the organization he founded. While Rida was committed to training small numbers of highly educated *ulama* who could in turn educate the wider public, al-Banna founded what was effectively a mass organization of lay preachers—or rather, given the Brotherhood's larger political agenda, lay activists. There was, for example, a student wing; a *nashr al-da'wa* (Department for Propagation of the Message), which trained *du'at* (missionaries) in public debating tactics; and a Department for Liaison with the Islamic World, with subcommittees devoted to different regions that reached as far as the United States, the Philippines, and, in a sign of remarkable ambition, the Pacific.

These developments marked an important step in the evolution of global Islam, not only in adding a revolutionary political current, but also in drawing religious authority further away from the *ulama*. After all, al-Banna was a government schoolteacher with no formal religious qualifications. His Brotherhood formed an alternative and well-organized hierarchy to counter that of the traditional Sufi-*ulama*.

An Indian *madrasa*'s missionary offspring

At the same time that al-Banna was building his band of brothers in Cairo, a quite different—and nonpolitical—organization was being established in Delhi. This was the Tablighi Jamaat (Preaching Society), founded in 1927 after Muhammad Ilyas (1885–1944) returned home from the *hajj*.

Ilyas was a graduate of the influential reformist seminary founded at Deoband in northern India back in 1866. Faced with the reality of colonial power, the Dar al-Ulum (House of Religious Sciences), as the Deoband *madrasa* was called, did not teach its students to rebel (though some did become anti-British activists). Instead, it promoted the practice of self-segregation from an impious wider society, which in India comprised local Hindus and Sikhs as well as Christians. In the absence of Muslim political power, Deobandi doctrine held that Sharia should be implemented at the personal and then, incrementally, the community level. Students who graduated from Deoband thus promoted the painstaking implementation of Sharia into the smallest details of daily life.

Like Salafis, Deoband graduates also rejected the shrines and rituals of the Sufis as godless *bid'at* (innovations) that led Muslims astray. But unlike Salafis, they maintained what they regarded as the higher doctrines of the Sufis, which they saw as comprising a path to moral perfection. However, these Sufi teachings were not to be made available to ordinary people—only to those trained first to follow scripture and Sharia.

Since its foundation, the *madrasa* at Deoband had adopted more efficient European classroom, curriculum, and examination methods to train hundreds of *ulama*. It also made effective use of print and post, issuing reformist religious primers in a simplified version of the colonial Indian lingua franca of Urdu. Back in 1892, the *madrasa* established a Dar al-Ifta (House of Rulings) that mailed *fatwas* (Sharia-based opinions) in reply to public requests about what was permitted or forbidden in Islam.

By the 1920s, hundreds of Deoband graduates had founded an extensive network of *madrasas* all over India and were expanding overseas into South Africa, challenging the authority of Sufi masters who a generation earlier had followed Indian indentured laborers to Natal. After the Second World War, under the chancellorship of Qari Muhammad Tayib (1897–1983), Deoband's model of self-replication and expansion through graduates founding their own *madrasas* would enable its influence to spread to other world regions, as we will see later.

But Muhammad Ilyas had no intention of founding a *madrasa*. The Tablighi Jamaat that he founded in 1927 created a more rapid and effective method of spreading Deobandi Islam that didn't require years of study in a seminary. Instead, it educated its members in simple Deoband-based tenets and then sent them on self-funded preaching tours. The Tablighi Jamaat began as a small grassroots organization sending such *jama'ats* (assemblies) of around a dozen members on *khuruj* (proselytizing tours) around India. In what was an extremely effective and low-cost model of expanding its influence, members were expected to devote themselves to preaching three nights each month, a continuous 40-day period each year, and a longer 120-day period at least once in their lifetimes, preferably overseas.

Ilyas had effectively invented a form of Islamic evangelicalism according to which it was a core duty of every Muslim to actively preach Islam—or rather, the Deobandi version of Islam. As with the Muslim Brotherhood, his followers were not trained *ulama* (and certainly not Sufis), but everyday Muslims, male and female, who pledged to follow the strict moral and behavioral code that emanated from Deoband. Their instantly recognizable dress code consisted of modest clothing they believed was favored by the Prophet and his wives.

Ultimately, the alliance with the Tablighi Jamaat represented a compromise for the Deobandi *ulama*, since as a lay preacher organization it undermined the authority of the *ulama* that the Deoband *madrasa* had been established to promote. Moreover, the Tablighis also watered down the complex, multilevel conception of Islam that the Deobandi *ulama* hoped to preserve. This was particularly the case with the importance the Deobandi *ulama* lent to Sufi *bay'at* (initiation) and *suhbat* (companionship) for advanced graduates, which the simplifying mass outreach model of the Tablighis would gradually undermine.

However, Ilyas did uphold the original Deobandi separation of Islam from politics. In contrast to the political travails that the Muslim Brotherhood was to face, this decision would allow his Tablighi Jamaat to expand without state persecution, whether in colonial India or the many other regions of the world to which its roving preachers would subsequently travel.

A Sufism adapted for the West

By the 1920s, Tablighis, Salafis, and various other Muslim reformists were attacking the Sufi foundations of world Islam as deviations from the Islam of scripture. At the same time, new nationalist and socialist regimes began closing Sufi institutions as spreaders of backwardness. Yet it was during this very period that Sufism found its first followers in a Europe and America disillusioned by Western civilization in the wake of the First World War.

We previously saw the Indian Inayat Khan and the Swedish convert Ivan Aguéli establishing short-lived Sufi circles in

London, Paris, and San Francisco during the 1910s and '20s, which gained a few hundred followers. The family and followers of Inayat Khan continued his International Sufi Movement after his death in 1927, with representatives appointed in areas as distant as Switzerland, the Netherlands, the United States, and Brazil, each winning small circles of Western followers. As for the assorted European occultists whom Aguéli initiated in Paris, the most influential was René Guénon (Abd al-Wahid Yahya, 1886–1951), who would introduce Sufism to a new generation of European intellectuals.

In the 1920s, another channel to Europe was opened from colonial North Africa by disciples of the Algerian Sufi master Ahmad al-Alawi (1869–1934), who had recently widened his following by launching a newspaper called *al-Balagh al-Jaza'iri* (Algerian Messenger) and giving the opening sermon at the Grand Mosque of Paris. In 1925, his brotherhood spread to Britain through one of the Yemeni sailors who settled in Cardiff, Wales, from where his following spread among the other Yemenis who constituted Britain's earliest Muslim community. Then, in 1933, after hearing about al-Alawi from Arab sailors in Marseilles, the Swiss esotericist Frithjof Schuon (1907–98) was initiated by him in Algeria. From there, Schuon returned to Europe to adapt al-Alawi's teachings for small audiences of non-Muslims.

The likes of Schuon, Aguéli, Guénon, and their subsequent Swiss follower Titus Burckhardt (1908–84) were not only fascinated by Sufism. They were also deeply interested in Theosophy, occultism, and Eastern religions in general. As a result, the version of Sufism they developed for their followers blended influences from a range of other spiritual and occult traditions. Often this came at the expense of more traditionally Islamic elements, particularly the observance of Sharia. In some cases, this led to the detaching of Sufism from Islam, unintentionally affirming the Salafi view that Sufism was never Islamic to begin with.

As this "de-Islamized" Sufism spread among unconventional freethinkers in places like San Francisco and Paris, its religious content was transformed, often abandoning any requirement to convert to Islam. In its European and American enclaves, this new Western Sufism was reared in protected isolation from its growing number of enemies in the Middle East and Asia. This pattern of disengagement would continue in the postwar decades when Muslim migrant populations began to settle in Europe. Part of the reason was the strong sense among Western Sufis that they were members of a spiritual avant-garde, which prevented them from entertaining any ambitions of becoming a mass movement. Very few of their works were translated into Arabic or other Muslim languages.

Meanwhile, Sufi masters in the Middle East and Asia were unwilling or unable to transform their brotherhoods into mass missionary movements. Wedded to their traditional brotherhood structures, they were also under fire from their ascendant critics. But there were a few exceptions, such as the All-Malaya Muslim Missionary Society, established in 1932 in Singapore by the Indian Sufi Abdul Aleem Siddiqi (1892–1954). Over the next twenty years, Siddiqi went on dozens of preaching tours as far as the Caribbean, even delivering the opening sermon for the second mosque in Japan, in Nagoya. He also published an English journal, *Genuine Islam*. But his Sufi mission was largely a one-man show and shrank after his death as independent Singapore clamped down on transnational Islamic activism.

Overall, the interwar period did not see the founding of any consequential Sufi counterweights to the anti-Sufi Muslim Brotherhood and Tablighi Jamaat. Many Sufis were in any case too preoccupied with defending their home ground from their critics to focus on proselytizing elsewhere. Although in their old rural heartlands other Sufis remained linchpins of world Islam, and in small Western enclaves they contributed a slender Sufi strand to global Islam, from the 1930s they were losing out to their detractors in the wider world.

The collective power of congresses

The interwar period saw other new mechanisms emerge besides the Muslim Brotherhood to organize Islam for political purposes. The inspiration came not only from the exemplary role played by Christian missionary societies, but also from the non-Muslim model of the League of Nations.

Between 1924 and 1935, five global Islamic congresses took place in Cairo, Mecca, Jerusalem, and Geneva (the headquarters of the League of Nations). The congresses were organized in response to the consequences of the First World War, particularly the end of the Ottoman caliphate, the Saudi-Wahhabi conquest of Mecca, and the British mandate over Palestine. After Japan's third mosque opened in Tokyo in 1938, the Greater Japan Muslim League organized another World Muslim Congress, with delegates drawn from across East and Southeast Asia. The congresses provided the solo activists of the age of empire with new forms of networking, organizing, and campaigning—in short, with a means of collective empowerment.

While the congresses were by no means straightforwardly Salafi or Deobandi affairs, such views were better represented than those of the traditional Sufi-*ulama* of world Islam. The central figure of the 1926 Congress of the Islamic World was King Ibn Saud (1875–1953), the Wahhabi founder of Saudi Arabia, while the main organizer of the 1931 General Islamic Congress was Hajj Amin al-Husseini (1897–1974), a Palestinian follower of Rashid Rida and holder of the influential post of Grand Mufti of Jerusalem who later worked with Nazi Germany. More moderate participants included the aging Lebanese impresario of Islamic unity Shakib Arslan, who organized the European Muslim Congress in Geneva, and critics of traditional Sufi masters such as

Sir Muhammad Iqbal (1877–1938), a celebrity delegate at the Jerusalem Congress. A graduate of Cambridge and Heidelberg, Iqbal tried to persuade the congress to found a new kind of Islamic university in Jerusalem that would educate Muslims from all over the world.

None of the interwar congresses achieved its core goals, whether of electing a new caliph, ejecting the British from Palestine, or founding an international university. Nor did they create permanent organizations. But by way of influential networks and models for transnational collective action, they left a major legacy to the postcolonial world order, which would see enduring Muslim intergovernmental organizations established in the 1960s. As we shall see, the founding of Islamic universities became one of their priorities.

Interwar Shi'i internationalism

During the interwar period, European control of the former Ottoman territories in the Middle East inadvertently helped Twelver Shi'i *ulama* further consolidate their authority. Together with the colonial transport and financial mechanisms discussed earlier, the removal of Ottoman Sunni preeminence enabled senior *ulama* to expand their influence from Najaf in British-mandated Iraq to Shi'i communities in French-mandated Lebanon and British-ruled India. Even so, no new Shi'i missionary or political organizations emerged to rival the Sunni likes of the Tablighi Jamaat or Muslim Brotherhood.

Arguably, the reason was that Shi'i *ulama* were too preoccupied with defending their largest stronghold in Iran. Despite having spent the last four centuries as the stronghold of Shi'i Islam, Iran had followed Ataturk's Turkey in embracing secularizing nationalism. After the coronation of Reza Shah Pahlavi in 1925, financial, judicial, and educational reforms were set in motion that removed Shi'i *ulama* from the positions of power they had previously enjoyed in Iran. At the same time elsewhere, the growing number of Salafi publications became highly critical of Shi'ism, denouncing its followers as apostates for their veneration of the twelve imams whom Shi'is believe succeeded the Prophet. Even more vociferous were the Wahhabi *ulama* associated with newly formed Saudi Arabia, itself home to an increasingly marginalized Shi'i minority. All in all, Twelver Shi'ism faced a series of challenges, even in its most populous domain in Iran, where official Pahlavi secularist policies cracked down on every aspect of religious influence. These policies contrasted strongly with the religious laissez-faire politics of the British, which allowed the Muslim Brotherhood and Tablighi Jamaat to expand across Egypt and India.

Elsewhere in the late British Empire, Indian donations were channeled to Shi'i *ulama* in British-administered Iraq. But during the 1920s and '30s, it was the minority Ismaili Shi'i followers of the Aga Khan line of *imams* who were in a more comfortable position than the Twelver Shi'i ulama, whether in Iran or Iraq. As these Ismailis expanded their business connections during the final phase of British imperial rule, their imam, Sir Sultan Muhammed Shah Aga Khan III (1877–1957), made personal visits to deepen his ties to this expansive trade diaspora. Following his first visit to British East Africa back in 1899, together with the various Ismaili benevolent societies, Aga Khan III funded numerous *jama'at khanas* (prayer houses), schools, and other welfare institutions across the Ismaili diaspora from Uganda to Burma. After relocating from Bombay to London and then Geneva, in 1932 Aga Khan III was nominated to represent India at the League of Nations, then appointed the league's overall president in 1937. But rather than promote his own version of Islam against its increasingly anti-Shi'i rivals, he preferred to promote the cause of inter-Muslim solidarity, hoping to play down the differences between his own followers and other Muslims.

The leaders of the Bohras, the other main Ismaili Muslim community, were likewise able to consolidate their authority over their approximately one million followers who had spread similarly across the British Empire from India. Shifting to Bombay like the Aga Khan beforehand, the Bohra hereditary leader Syedna Taher Saifuddin (1888–1965) used his tightly knit community's trade networks to collect tithes that were redistributed as social welfare. This made his office ever more central to community life. Connected like his contemporary Aga Khan III to the institutions of late empire, Saifuddin served as chancellor of India's elite Aligarh Muslim University. Printing a new epistle every year that sought to reconcile Bohra tradition with the modern world, Saifuddin succeeded in upholding his hereditary authority as *da'i al-mutlaq* (absolute leader), which he then passed on to his son.

Like the other Ismaili branch that followed the Aga Khan— indeed, like Shi'i religious leaders more generally—the traditional Bohra leadership managed to maintain its position. Nevertheless, they did so at the cost of not trying to expand their authority over other Muslims. Even though the Bohra and Aga Khani Ismailis founded their own community mosques, schools, and welfare associations throughout the British Empire, they founded no program of *da'wa* or *tabligh* (propagation) that would promote Ismailism as a global rival to Salafism or Deobandism. Yet by not developing expansive "lay preacher" organizations, both Ismaili and Twelver Shi'ism were largely able to maintain the religious authority of their imam or *da'i* (in the Ismaili case) and *ulama* (in the Twelver case).

In subsequent decades, this would help Shi'ism avoid the large-scale fragmentation experienced by Sunnism that resulted from the emergence of so many new Sunni religious activists and organizations.

In the wake of the Second World War

In the decolonizing postwar world, Islam became increasingly irrelevant at the level of international politics except insofar as it could be promoted as a bulwark against communism as the Cold War took hold in the 1950s. From Egypt to India and Malaysia, postcolonial states promoted secular nationalism, while the People's Republic of China and southeastern Europe joined the Soviet Union in promoting socialist atheism. In many regions of the world, this spectrum between state indifference and outright state hostility limited the ability of global Islamic activists and organizations to travel, network, fundraise, publish, or simply proselytize.

Consequently, the postwar period up to around 1970 saw global Islam rerouted owing to the closing of borders around China, the Soviet Union, and the Eastern Bloc, as well as various Soviet-aligned socialist states in Africa and Asia. No longer an imperial power, postwar Japan also dropped off the map of global Islam. However, in less hostile nationalist settings, such as Egypt and Indonesia, Muslim religious organizations not only survived but continued to win supporters, partly by learning to speak the acceptable language of nationalism. As a result, various new national-level Islamic organizations were founded that served as regional channels for global Islam through the interaction of their members with transnational organizations such as the Jama'at-i Islami and new international organizations such as the World Muslim Congress, both discussed below. As conduits for global Salafism, these kinds of national organizations would prove particularly popular among growing urban populations, who were more susceptible to the modernizing and moralizing dimensions of their message. This was particularly true after 1970 as corrupt or inept secular politicians failed to deliver on their promises.

The geography of global Islam was thus not fixed. In the 1950s and '60s, geopolitics again shaped its redistribution in a way that allowed the networks forged in previous periods to cohere around two new global Islamic hubs in quite different political environments.

The first of these new environments comprised the two exceptions to the secularizing postcolonial trend, namely Pakistan and Saudi Arabia. The second comprised the liberal democracies of western Europe, and to some extent the United States, whose rules regarding religious freedom made them attractive sanctuaries for a range of religious activists and organizations, not least those persecuted by nationalists at home.

A Muslim United Nations

In a postwar world dominated at the state level by secularizing politics, the founding of Pakistan in 1947 and the petrodollar enrichment of Saudi Arabia beginning in the 1960s allowed states to reemerge as important sponsors of global Islam for the first time since the collapse of the Ottoman caliphate in 1924.

In 1949, Pakistan oversaw the establishment of the World Muslim Congress (Motamar al-'Alam al-Islami), modeled as the antithesis of the secular international institutions promoted by the United Nations, founded four years earlier. Other transnational Muslim assemblies followed, a proliferation partly fueled by rivalries with other states that hoped to instrumentalize Islamic causes such as the earlier Ottoman promoters of Islamic unity. Basing the World Muslim Congress in Karachi gave Pakistan particular advantages: the Congress was effectively run by Pakistani officials.

In 1962, the Saudi Arabian government responded by founding the Mecca-based Rabita al-'Alam al-Islami (Muslim World League). Two years later, nationalist Egypt responded by sponsoring international conferences in Cairo via its state-run Academy of Islamic Researches. Not to be outdone, in 1967 the Ismaili imam Prince Karim al-Hussaini Aga Khan IV established the Aga Khan Foundation, based, like many UN agencies, in Geneva.

All of these organizations sought to foster Muslim worldwide unity, albeit on quite different terms. So while the Aga Khan Foundation was determinedly nonsectarian (as a tiny Shi'i minority the Ismailis had more to lose than win by denouncing their Sunni neighbors), the Pakistan-based World Muslim Congress and particularly the Saudi-based Muslim World League promoted more sectarian versions of global Islam. The Muslim World League became a powerful umbrella sponsor of all manner of worldwide Salafi-Wahhabi initiatives and organizations. By contrast, there were no state-sponsored organizations promoting or even defending Sufi Islam on a global scale.

A few states, such as republican Egypt and monarchical Morocco, sought to maintain the old Sufi-*ulama* establishment, and individual Sufis certainly attended conferences at al-Azhar and the World Muslim Congress. But their influence was diluted by the Muslim World League's promotion of Salafi-Wahhabism with the rich proceeds of Saudi oil revenues.

Organizing Saudi ascendancy

By the early 1960s, the Muslim World League was only one of several mechanisms by which Saudi Arabia began exporting Salafi-Wahhabism worldwide as a counterforce to communism and Arab nationalism.

Prior to the Saudi conquests of the 1920s, the holy cities of Mecca and Medina had served as an important hub for the Sufi-*ulama* who moved around the Indian Ocean. But with the consolidation of Saudi rule, the Sufis institutions in Mecca were closed and Sufi influence was replaced by the combined forces of the Salafi acolytes of Rashid Rida and the Wahhabi allies of the House of Saud.

In 1961, this development went a step further with the opening of the Islamic University of Madinah (IUM). From 1970, the leading Wahhabi scholar Abd al-Aziz bin Abdullah bin Baz (1910–99) effectively ran it, first as vice president and then as president. (He was also later president of the Muslim World League). The IUM served as a transnational seminary for the dissemination of Salafi-Wahhabism, its activities guided by an Advisory Council of leading Salafis from Egypt, Syria, Iraq, Tunisia, Mauritania, India, and Indonesia, as well as prominent members of the Syrian Muslim Brotherhood and the Pakistani Jama'at-i Islami. The faculty comprised a similarly international crowd, many of them also distinguished Salafis. More than 80 percent of its entirely male student body came from outside Saudi Arabia on scholarships that covered tuition, travel, and living expenses. After graduating, many returned to their home regions, where the prestige they had acquired by studying in Medina led them to be appointed imams of mosques, heads of national religious associations, and founders of schools and organizations of their own.

Another means of exporting Salafi-Wahhabism came through the *hajj*. As we saw earlier, since 1928 compulsory escorts called *mutawwif* (guides) or *mu'alim* (teachers) were trained to inculcate Salafi-Wahhabi principles in pilgrims to Mecca. The confluence of increasingly cheap air travel and Saudi policies of religious diplomacy saw the annual number of overseas *hajjis* leap from 150,000 to 700,000 between the 1950s and the 1970s. They came from almost every country in the world, including, from 1968, the Soviet Union.

By these varied methods, the teachings of the formerly obscure Wahhabi *ulama* of the Arabian backwater of Najd were exported across the globe.

Proselytizing from the Land of the Pure

The other key postwar state promoter of global Islamic activists and organizations was Pakistan. This occurred not only through the Karachi-based World Muslim Congress, but also through a series of nongovernmental organizations (NGOs) that gained increasing influence as Pakistan's postcolonial polity and society searched for an identity and purpose.

A new type of state, its name—meaning "the Land of the Pure"—had been coined in 1933 by an Indian Muslim student at Cambridge. The country's cultured colonial Indian founders had envisaged a secular state where liberal and even democratic versions of Islam could flourish through a postcolonial Muslim renaissance. But as early as the 1950s, the nature of the Islam that the Pakistani state was meant to promote came to be highly contested. Matters were further complicated by the fact that Pakistan's ruling elite were mostly secular figures who lacked any claim to religious authority. This conundrum gradually led secular state officials into a series of compromises and collusions with religious organizations, whose influence became increasingly hard to contain. In 1973, the third Constitution of Pakistan declared the country an Islamic Republic, whose laws should "be brought in conformity with the injunctions of Islam as laid down in the Holy Quran and Sunnah."

Pakistan also became an increasingly important hub for the missionary Tablighi Jamaat. Although formed in Delhi in 1927, in the decades after independence in 1947, the Pakistani railway junction town of Raiwind became its global headquarters. From Pakistan, the Tablighi Jamaat spread widely, first by preaching along the pilgrimage routes to Mecca and then on the Arabian Peninsula itself. At the same time, missions were sent to Egypt, Sudan, Syria, Turkey, Afghanistan, Malaysia, Burma, Indonesia, East Africa, Britain, the United States, and Japan. In 1961, the first Tablighi missions were sent to mainland Europe and West Africa, exporting their simplified version of Deobandi Islam far from its place of origin.

Within a few decades of sending the first preaching parties to Lagos in 1960, the Tablighi Jamaat established more than three

7. In the small Indian railway town of Deoband, the Dar al-Ulum seminary trained *ulama* who went on to found a global network of Deobandi madrasas.

hundred centers in Nigeria alone. Tablighi influence even managed to breach the Iron Curtain via Soviet student exchange programs. After studying in Deobandi seminaries in India, the Uzbekistan-born Damullah Hindustani (1892–1989), for example, established secret study circles on his return to Soviet central Asia.

Mobile vanguards of the call for revolution

While the Tablighi Jamaat promoted a nonpolitical version of Islam (at least at the level of state politics), Pakistan also hosted the Jama'at-i Islami (Islamic Society), which was devoted to establishing an international Islamic state.

The Jama'at-i Islami was founded in 1941 in India by Abul A'la Maududi (1903–79), who subsequently shifted the group's headquarters to Pakistan to challenge the new country's secular founders. Like Hasan al-Banna, the founder of the Muslim Brotherhood, Maududi was not a trained member of the *ulama*. Rather, he was a journalist who learned the value of mass media through his participation in the campaign to save the Ottoman caliphate. In 1933, he founded his Urdu journal, *Tarjuman al-Quran* (Interpreter of the Quran), which publicized his ideas for the rest of his life. He also wrote many short books and the six-volume *Tafhim al-Quran* (Understanding the Quran), which claimed that the scriptures urged Muslims to struggle for the foundation of an Islamic state.

Maududi presented the Quran as a political textbook centrally concerned with the concept of *hakimiyya* (sovereignty). Since legitimate sovereignty can only be divinely ordained, it requires states run in accordance with Sharia. According to Maududi, the installation of divine sovereignty was perpetually undermined by *shirk*, a Quranic term that traditionally meant idolatry but that he expanded to include all opposition to divine rule, which is to say, to the foundation of an Islamic state. Moreover, since divine sovereignty is indivisible, like the deity himself, such a state must likewise be a single, worldwide one. By this reasoning, nation-states that failed to implement Sharia served only to further perpetuate *shirk*, even if they were controlled by nominal Muslims, so the duty of every Muslim was to oppose them with every ounce of their being. For Maududi, the Quran provided the commandments and lessons for how to do so, via violent jihad if necessary. This notion of jihad as political struggle formed the basis of Maududi's transformation of Islam into an ideology—that is, into an explanatory program towards a defined political goal.

For all his talk of returning to the core teachings of the Quran, Maududi was deeply influenced by the global political currents of his time. He borrowed key political concepts, such as the notion of an *inqilab* (revolution) led by a *giroh* (vanguard), from the lexicon of the Indian Marxists he encountered during his years as a journalist. Having come of age under British rule over India, he also shared the antipathy to the imperialist West of his Marxist contemporaries, though, like al-Banna, he sought to replace Western hegemony with state-implemented Sharia. After moving to Pakistan and transforming the Jama'at-i Islami into a transnational political party, he came to regard Asian and Middle Eastern nationalists as the divisive enemies of his global Islamic revolution.

As a result of his revolutionary activism, Maududi found himself repeatedly imprisoned by the Pakistani authorities and even sentenced to death. But the compromises of Pakistani secularism saw Maududi no less frequently pardoned and released, leaving him free to travel and lecture worldwide. Propelled by the expansion of passenger air travel, during the 1950s and '60s his lecture tours took in the Middle East, North Africa, western Europe, and North America. In 1961, he was welcomed to Saudi Arabia as one of the founders of the Islamic University of Madinah. Meanwhile, his revolutionary writings were translated into dozens of languages by the Jama'at-i Islami's Translation Bureau in Lahore. By 1974, his *Risala-yi Diniyat* (Towards Understanding Islam) had appeared in twenty-six languages.

Maududi's Jama'at-i Islami organization magnified his influence by a range of other mechanisms besides publishing. Echoing the evolution of the Muslim Brotherhood in Egypt, the Jama'at-i Islami expanded its urban following in Pakistan through educational and social welfare programs. Then, like the Tablighi Jamaat, it turned its attention overseas. In 1962, the United Kingdom Islamic Mission was formed. Initially based at the East London Mosque, it mirrored the Jama'at-i Islami's model of providing social welfare services to Pakistani and later Bangladeshi migrants while making Maududi's works available for free or at nominal cost in the emerging mosques and Muslim bookstores of Britain. Its offshoot, the Islamic Foundation, established in Leicestershire in 1973, specialized in distributing Maududi's writings on a larger, international scale.

The Jama'at-i Islami's strategy of reaching out to migrant Muslims to "rediscover" their faith, albeit in a highly politicized and sectarian version, would later be expanded to other world regions. Although only a small minority of Muslim migrants followed Maududi, the Jama'at-i Islami nonetheless gave him one of global Islam's loudest voices in the postcolonial era.

Brothers in exile

Via translations into Arabic, Maududi's ideas were also taken up in Egypt by members of the Muslim Brotherhood. But after its spectacular growth in the late colonial period, in the nationalizing postwar decades the Brotherhood entered a period of wandering in the wilderness.

In 1949, its founder, Hasan al-Banna, had been killed (likely by Egyptian security forces), after one of his followers assassinated the Egyptian prime minister. This initiated a period of government suppression that worsened between 1954 and 1970 under the nationalist rule of Gamal Abdel Nasser. After its weekly newspaper, *al-Da'wa* (Proselytizing), was closed in 1956, the Brotherhood was forced to operate clandestinely, training lecturers to spread its revolutionary ideas under the guise of nonpolitical piety and social welfare.

By this time the Brotherhood had already spread through the Arab Middle East. But the postwar decades also saw it find members and imitators in other countries where it was not banned. New branches were first established in other Arabic-speaking countries, including in Africa, where the Brotherhood's outreach to students in Sudan saw it recruit Hasan Abdullah al-Turabi (1932–2016), who we will later see transforming his country into an Islamic state.

Meanwhile, as the continued prestige of the medieval seminary of al-Azhar brought students to Cairo from as far away as Nigeria and Indonesia, some were exposed to al-Banna's teachings through covert study circles dedicated to what was by then a widely available backlist of Brotherhood publications. Among these foreign students was a young Afghan called Burhanuddin Rabbani (1940–2011), who arrived in Cairo in 1966. While completing his doctoral degree in Islamic studies, he quietly immersed himself in the teachings of al-Banna and Maududi. Rabbani returned home to an influential post as professor of Islamic studies at Kabul University, where he disseminated the ideas of al-Banna and Maududi among his own students. In 1972 he became the first leader of the Jama'at-i Islami of Afghanistan. This was part of a larger pattern of the transnational replication of organizations dedicated to the revolutionary installation of Islamic states.

However, brutal suppression in the Muslim Brotherhood's home base in Egypt encouraged some members to seek refuge in Europe and establish Brotherhood-modeled organizations there. This process began in the early 1960s via the efforts of al-Banna's personal secretary and son-in-law, Said Ramadan (1926–95). Already a seasoned international activist, Ramadan had fought in Palestine among Arab volunteers and founded a branch of the Brotherhood in Jerusalem. He now applied for the office of secretary general of the Pakistan-based World Muslim Congress, which drew him to Karachi. There he ran an influential Salafi-inspired radio program while networking with Maududi and his Jama'at-i Islami. Between 1952 and 1955, Ramadan used his experience with the Brotherhood to help Maududi's followers organize their own student wing, the Islami Jama'at-i Tulabah (Islamic Students Association). Through campus protests and publications such as the English-language *Student's Voice*, the Jama'at-i Islami's student wing spread political Islam among the younger generation in Pakistan and then among Muslim students elsewhere, including Bangladesh and Britain.

Ramadan's next outpost was Germany. Ostensibly he went there to study at the University of Cologne, but practically he needed to escape Nasser's crackdown in Egypt. However, he soon moved on to Geneva, a favorite vacation destination of wealthy Saudis, and with their support he obtained a Saudi diplomatic passport. Geneva became the Brotherhood's first outpost in Europe when Ramadan founded an Islamic Center there in 1961. Via this institutional transplant, he set about organizing other Brotherhood members who had fled to Europe, as well as drawing new recruits among the many Arab and other Muslim students (often learning technical subjects) being sponsored through postcolonial state-building programs.

A major milestone was reached with Ramadan's takeover of a mosque-building committee in Munich. Saudi funding enabled him to marginalize the Tatar migrants who had come to Germany from Russia, where they had previously been influenced by the modernist Jadids of the Russian Empire. After securing the Brotherhood's control of the new Munich mosque, Ramadan established the Islamische Gemeinschaft in Deutschland (German Islamic Society). This turn sponsored a growing network of Brotherhood-controlled mosques, Islamic centers, and "cultural associations" (which faced fewer legal restrictions) that spread first across West Germany and then throughout western Europe at large.

North America also now fell within the Brotherhood's purview. In 1963, Arab members of the Brotherhood studying at the University of Illinois were allegedly involved in forming a Muslim student organization.

Ramadan was helped by several other activists, including the wealthy Egyptian businessmen who would later help found the bank widely believed to be a channel for transferring Saudi and other Persian Gulf–state funding to Brotherhood offshoots in Europe and America. To some degree, Ramadan and his brothers-in-exile were also supported by the CIA as a counterforce to anti-American Arab nationalism, though not to anything like the extent claimed by conspiracy theorists.

While the fortunate likes of Ramadan settled in Switzerland, thousands of Muslim Brothers remained imprisoned in Egypt. But even from behind bars, one of them would have massive influence, both on the Brotherhood and the politicization of global Islam more generally. This was Sayyid Qutb (1906–66) who, like al-Banna, was not a *madrasa*-trained member of the *ulama* but a secular schoolteacher. Qutb developed his ideas through interactions with the non-Muslim world via a government scholarship to attend a teacher training college in Greeley, Colorado. It was there, amid the mixing of the sexes, pop music, and consumerism of postwar America, that he abandoned his earlier vocation of writing novels to produce his first religious work, *al-ʿAdala al-Ijtima'iya fi al-Islam* (Social Justice in Islam).

Returning to Egypt and reading Arabic translations of Maududi, Qutb joined the Brotherhood, rapidly rising to its Guidance Council and serving as its Director of Propagation. Among other ideas, he took from Maududi the reinterpretation of the Quranic idea of the *jahiliya* (age of ignorance). For Maududi and now Qutb, *jahiliya* meant not only the distant past before Muhammad's revelation; the age of ignorance was also the present day, when secularism and nationalism had led Muslims astray to the point that it was necessary to use violent struggle by way of jihad to lead people back to God's way, as the Prophet had in Maududi's and now Qutb's eyes.

After being imprisoned on account of a plot to assassinate President Nasser, from his prison cell Qutb wrote his two most influential works, *Fi Zilal al-Quran* (In the Shade of the Quran, 1954) and *Maʿalim fi al-Tariq* (Milestones, 1964). Couched in the rich prose style he had first mastered as a novelist inspired by leading European authors, his works blended humanitarian empathy for the plight of fellow Muslims with a radically politicized version of the Salafi return to the commands of scripture. For Qutb, anyone opposed to the revolutionary establishment of Sharia-based government was an enemy of Islam. By vastly expanding the concept of *takfir* (declaring a fellow Muslim an apostate), even Muslims could legitimately be killed in the long-drawn-out jihad required to bring about Qutb's Salafi utopia.

Although many members of the Brotherhood subsequently rejected Qutb, together with Maududi he served as the chief global theorist of jihad as the mechanism for establishing Islamic states.

From Sunni to Shi'i revolutionaries

Having been targeted by vitriolic polemic from various Wahhabi- and Salafi-inspired authors, many Shi'i religious figures shunned the Muslim Brotherhood. But in the cause of Muslim unity in the shared campaign against secularism, some mid-century *ulama* based in Cairo, Qom, and Najaf sought to bridge the Sunni–Shi'i divide by promoting the doctrine of *taqrib* (reconciliation).

Originally promoted by the Jama'at al-Taqrib (Society for Reconciliation), which was active in Egypt during the late 1940s, the doctrine was later taken up by a range of other thinkers, whether for political or ecumenical purposes. This well-intentioned détente inadvertently allowed revolutionary ideas to spread from Egypt to the Shi'i circles of Iraq and Iran. As early as 1953, Sayyid Qutb held meetings in Cairo with Navvab Safavi (1924–56), the Iranian leader of the Fada'iyan-i Islam (Self-Sacrificers of Islam), which was founded in 1946 and began assassinating secular government officials soon thereafter. By the 1960s, the ideological and organizational innovations of the Muslim Brothers were being watched with keen interest by a younger generation of marginalized, and in some cases exiled, Shi'i *ulama* in Iran and Iraq, as well as angry young activists in secular but autocratic Afghanistan.

Among the many translations of Qutb's works were those into Persian by the aforementioned Afghan Burhanuddin Rabbani (subsequent president of the Islamic State of Afghanistan) and the Iranian Ayatullah Ali Khamenei (subsequent supreme leader of the Islamic Republic of Iran). These and other such mechanisms allowed Qutb's ideas to begin crossing both spatial and sectarian boundaries to influence Shi'is in Pahlavi Iran and Baathist Iraq who faced the same threats from secular nationalist governments.

The 1960s also saw Maududi's works translated by other Shi'i *ulama*, such as Hadi Khosrowshahi. In 1969, the Iranian political exile Ruhollah Khomeini (1902–89), who was closely affiliated with these translators in Iraq, wrote a work titled *Hukumat-i Islami* (Islamic Government). This key text would transfer Maududi and Qutb's concept of an Islamic revolution from Pakistan and Egypt to the Shi'i setting of Iran, where in 1979 Khomeini would lead an Islamic revolution of the kind Maududi had first theorized.

Meanwhile, Qutb's ideas were influencing Shi'is in Iraq, where Muhammad Baqir al-Sadr (1935–80) emerged as the leading figure of the Hizb al-Da'wa al-Islamiyya (Islamic Propagation Party). Founded in 1958, the organization opposed Iraq's ruling secularists, particularly the Arab socialists of the Ba'ath party, who had seized power that year. Under pressure at home, Hizb al-Da'wa members soon sought refuge in Kuwait, the United Arab Emirates, and Lebanon. In exile, Hizb al-Da'wa founded seminaries to train the younger generation in this new political Shi'ism. In the early 1970s around a hundred members settled in Lebanon, laying the foundation for groups such as Hezbollah (Party of God) that would emerge during the Lebanese civil war (1975–90).

In 1964, the new political Islam also reached Lebanon's Sunni Muslims with the founding of the Jama'a al-Islamiyya (Islamic Society), a breakaway organization from the Muslim Brotherhood.

Sufi nonpolitical alternatives

In the background to these developments, traditional Sufi masters continued to present themselves as charismatic living channels of divine grace and wisdom. Rural and inland regions of Africa and of South and Southeast Asia remained strongholds of Sufi-dominated world Islam. However, in urban environments especially, many Sufi leaders chose to compromise with the Salafi scripturalists and Deobandi legalists by abandoning some of their doctrines and ritual practices rather than publicly countering their critics. Struggling to maintain their home grounds, and in many cases having had their landholding endowments seized by nationalizing governments, Sufis formed no transnational equivalent to the Muslim Brotherhood or Tablighi Jamaat.

In one of the unexpected displacements of religious globalization, in precisely the period when its status was plummeting elsewhere, Sufism began winning more enthusiasts among non-Muslims in the West. In the 1960s, the writings of European Sufis such as the aforementioned René Guénon and Frithjof Schuon found a new readership among non-Muslim youths. With the help of the bohemian poet Robert Graves, the Scottish Indian author Idries Shah (1924–96) similarly began presenting the Sufis in ways that appealed to the countercultural movement. Yet none of these Western Sufis founded mass organizations; what organizations were founded remained confined to fringe circles in Europe and America.

Nonetheless, there were Sufi teachers who strenuously defended the Muslim foundations of Sufism, and some of them went to Europe on preaching tours. Among the most prominent of these transnational Sufi preachers were Pakistanis educated in the numerous Barelvi *madrasas* founded by followers of Ahmad Riza Khan Barelvi (1856–1921), who sought to defend Sufi devotional rituals from their critics. These Barelvi teachers competed with their Deobandi rivals for control of the many British mosques founded for migrants from South Asia. Similarly, the West African Mouridiyya brotherhood spread among the Senegalese diaspora in France. But in both cases, their immigrant followers moved in separate social circles from middle-class European Sufis, and they were unable to build common cause and solidarity in the way like-minded promoters of political Islam were learning to do.

As a result, during the half century that ended in 1970, the Sufi input into global Islam did not grow to anything like a degree comparable to that of their highly organized and state-funded detractors. Founded in 1967, the Maoist-inspired People's Democratic Republic of Yemen murdered Sufi leaders and destroyed their shrines and meeting houses, which had once attracted followers from all around the Indian Ocean. When Colonel Muammar Gaddafi seized power in Libya in 1969, he likewise banned the Sanusi Sufi brotherhood, whose hereditary leaders were also the ruling royal family, and persecuted its more prominent members.

Persecuted by socialist and nationalist states, and led by hereditary families with no incentive to revise the organizational status quo, the Sufi brotherhoods did not form any transnational organizations on the scale of their rivals with publishing, translation, and propagation departments. As a result, no twentieth-century Sufi's writings were circulated on a global scale comparable to that enjoyed by the multiply translated output of Qutb and Maududi; the latter, by contrast, lived just long enough to watch an Islamic revolution he helped inspire take place in Iran. Nonetheless, while the revolutionaries captured the headlines, they remained only one aspect of global Islam, albeit an increasingly powerful one.

Chapter 4
From Islamic revolutions to the Internet

Beginning in the 1970s, a series of seismic political developments empowered some global Islamic organizations more than others, while also creating the circumstances that afforded successful and failed attempts to establish Islamic states. Most influential were two interrelated changes in the geopolitical landscape. The first was the Islamic Revolution in Iran and the anti-Soviet jihad in Afghanistan, which contributed to the breakdown of the Soviet Union and the end of the Cold War. The second was the subsequent emergence of the neoliberal post-Soviet world order, which encouraged the opening of multiple borders after 124 governments joined the World Trade Organization in 1995.

While the doctrinal and organizational legacy of previous decades were passed on to this period, two further developments changed the infrastructure of global Islam in the half century after 1970. The first was the increasing role of states, particularly through the emergence of different types of Islamic state (broadly defined here as states that promote Sharia). The second was the spread of new transport and communication technologies via cheap air travel and first analog and then digital media by way of audiocassettes, satellite television, and the Internet. These technologies enabled even individual religious actors to reach global audiences far more easily and inexpensively than ever before. As much as they aided each other, these two developments were also frequently in tension, as states, NGOs, and individuals increasingly competed for religious authority.

The organizational forms of global Islam also evolved, taking inspiration as before from non-Muslim models. In contexts of expanding urban populations and underperforming economies in the Middle East, Asia, and Africa, the provision of public services became an important factor in the success of transnational Islamic NGOs. After the founding of the Jeddah-based Islamic Development Bank in 1975, the next decades also witnessed a spectacular expansion of Sharia-compliant financial institutions. In line with the hybridizing tendencies of globalization, both Islamic banks and NGOs formed Islamized counterparts to Western institutions.

Meanwhile, migration to Europe and North America created religiously underserved diaspora populations that attracted a host of global Islamic organizations. In western Europe, Muslim migrants largely comprised rural and small-town populations previously attached to regional forms of world Islam. Not only did resettlement in Europe detach them—and particularly their offspring—from their ancestral religious leaders, shrines, and customs, but it also removed their social support networks. Global Islamic organizations responded to the social and cultural dislocation of migration by seizing the opportunity to offer community support and representation centered in Islamic associations and mosques they controlled. Such organizations sought to replace migrants' commitments to the world Islam of their ancestors by offering rationalist, scripturalist, or political versions of Islam that appeared more sophisticated or authentic than "village religion." While such Muslim-heritage migrants were not synonymous with adherents of global Islam, they did form new population groups that global Islamic organizations competed to proselytize, with varying degrees of success.

The overall result was that global Islam again moved, finding new locations in places as dissimilar as post-Soviet central Asia and France, as well as what would emerge as the unruly virtual space of the Internet. All this exacerbated the ongoing fragmentation of religious authority.

The oil boom of Saudi Salafism

Since the crowning of King Faisal in 1964 at the height of the Arab nationalist movement, Islam had been increasingly instrumentalized through the Saudi foreign policy of *al-tadamun al-islami* (Islamic solidarity). Its main mechanisms were state-sponsored institutions such as the Mecca-based Muslim World League (and its many sub organizations) and the Islamic University of Madinah. After the oil boom of the early 1970s, their activities were massively expanded and joined by the efforts of several other Saudi-funded religious organizations.

8. Founded in 1961, the Islamic University of Madinah used growing Saudi oil revenues to offer scholarships to young Muslims from every part of the world.

These were the Organization of the Islamic Conference (since renamed the Organization of Islamic Cooperation) and the World Assembly of Muslim Youth, both founded in 1972. The following year, Saudi Arabia helped establish the Islamic Council of Europe, with headquarters in London, which channeled funding and influence to mosques and Islamic societies across Europe. Through policies aimed at other governments, such as agreements and loans, as well as at NGOs, along with Islamic institutes and colleges, many other Saudi-funded umbrella organizations exported Salafi-Wahhabism via its institutional replication overseas. Nonetheless, official Saudi religion was more politically conservative than revolutionary, though the influence of the Muslim Brotherhood in Saudi universities would in some places promote a more politicized version of Salafi-Wahhabism.

In 1976 grants and loans made by the Organization of the Islamic Conference to member states reached a shade under US$2 billion, while between 1975 and 1981 the Muslim World League considerably increased its budget earmarked for training imams, building mosques, and distributing texts in Africa. The oil boom of the 1970s allowed the annual budget of the Islamic University of Madinah to increase almost fivefold, expanding its international student body from under 600 to well over 2000 (and eventually over 20,000). These preachers-in-training were drawn now from Southeast Asia and West Africa as well as from neighboring Arabic-speaking countries and Europe. Meanwhile, from its headquarters in Riyadh, the richly funded World Assembly of Muslim Youth began promoting Salafi-Wahhabism among student organizations worldwide, including Europe and Southeast Asia.

The spread of cheap air travel that began in the 1970s exposed ever larger numbers of ordinary Muslims from more regions of the world to Salafi-Wahhabism as the normative Islam of Mecca. As the number of migrant workers in Saudi Arabia increased from around 300,000 in 1971 to nearly 2.5 million in 1979, on an incremental but extensive scale many returnees exported Saudi religious norms to their home regions, particularly India, Pakistan, and the Philippines.

Then, in the autumn of 1979, Saudi Arabia briefly lost control of its key religious asset: the Kaaba. On November 20, armed followers of a self-proclaimed Muslim *mahdi* (messiah) called Muhammad Abdullah al-Qahtani (1935–80) seized control of Islam's holiest mosque in Mecca under the leadership of Qahtani's brother-in-law, Juhayman al-Otaybi (1936–80). Thousands of pilgrims were initially trapped inside the compound. In the Islamic calendar, the date was Muharram 1, 1400: the first day of the new Islamic century. After the bloody end to the "Siege of Mecca," Saudi Arabia's rulers gave yet more resources to Salafi-Wahhabi institutions as a counterweight to such messianic deviancy. But an even greater religious threat to Saudi influence was emerging in the foundation of a revolutionary Islamic Republic in Iran, whose new theocratic constitution was approved in December 1979. As Iran increasingly claimed leadership over the world's Muslims, by 1986 this interstate competition would lead King Fahd (r. 1982–2005) to adopt the prestigious religious title Custodian of the Two Holiest Mosques (Khadim al-Haramayn al-Sharifayn).

Fueled by growing concerns with Iran and the ongoing struggle with Soviet socialism, which influenced a series of Muslim-majority socialist client states, Saudi Arabia's Islam-based foreign policy was remarkably wide-reaching. By the 1980s, the Mecca-based Muslim World League had even funneled Saudi influence into the remote islands of the Indian Ocean. In December 1984, the Saudi foreign minister visited the Comoros Islands, from where students would later be given scholarships for the Islamic University of Madinah; this led to the gradual ascendance of Sharia in the former French colony. In the Maldives, traditional wooden mosques and Sufi shrines were torn down and replaced with Gulf-style concrete structures. Saudi aid was also channeled to Muslims in multiethnic Mauritius, where the electoral success of the Hindu-supported Mouvement Socialiste Militant had led to the abolition of Muslim Personal Law. By the early 1990s the Salafi-oriented Zam Zam Islamic Center had been established in Mauritius, and the Saudi-educated Cehl Meeah (b. 1958) had launched his Hizbullah Party to counter the Hindu/socialist vote.

Much Saudi attention was also paid to Asia. In 1980, the International Islamic University of Islamabad was launched in the capital of Pakistan, which also hosted the similarly Saudi-funded Faisal Masjid, the largest in the mosque world when it was completed in 1986. Other Saudi-financed mosques and universities were inaugurated in Ghana and Malaysia, along with the Institute for the Study of Islam and Arabic in the Indonesian capital of Jakarta in 1980.

However, it was in Afghanistan that the Saudi struggle against socialism would reap its greatest geopolitical harvest as its sponsorship of a violent version of Salafism slipped increasingly out of its control.

The jihad against godless socialism

By distributing Qurans, building mosques, and promoting Muslim solidarity, Saudi Arabia was conducting its own Cold War. But the conflict turned very hot in the wake of the Saudi response to the Soviet invasion of Afghanistan in December 1979. Together with its American and European allies, Saudi Arabia was to make its most momentous contributions to the global transformation of Islam, which had unintended consequences for all parties concerned, none more than the Afghans. Yet even when Saudi officials began sponsoring Salafi-jihadists in Afghanistan, at home they promoted politically quietist Salafi-Wahhabis, such as Muhammad Nasir al-Din al-Albani (1914–99) and Rabi' al-Madkhali (b. 1931). Ironically, these contradictions would turn the Salafism that Rashid Rida had invented to unify Muslims around a simple common creed into a polemical and violent arena of internal conflict.

Until the early 1980s, the doctrines of Salafi-jihadism were limited to a persecuted and marginal group of Muslim Brothers and others inspired by the writings of Sayyid Qutb, who had been executed in Cairo back in 1966. But when local Afghans began to organize armed resistance to the Soviets, Saudi Arabia joined the United States and Pakistan in supplying money and weapons. Afghan Salafists such as Burhanuddin Rabbani and Abd al-Rasul Sayyaf, who had been exposed to the works of Qutb and other Muslim Brothers as students in Cairo, soon emerged as the key middlemen. Channeling funds together with ideological direction, they conceptualized the Afghan resistance as a revolutionary jihad in line with Qutb and Maududi's vision. As such, this was not to be a defensive struggle to reinstate the pre-Soviet status quo in Afghanistan, when Sufi-*ulama* had comprised Afghanistan's religious establishment. For some participants at least, it was a revolutionary struggle to establish an Islamic state.

By rendering the war an international Islamic rather than a narrowly nationalist campaign, up to 35,000 foreign volunteers were attracted to fight in Afghanistan. The globalizing trajectory of the Afghan jihad can be illustrated through the career of Abdullah Azzam (1941–89). Born in Palestine, where he was introduced to the Muslim Brotherhood as a youth, Azzam studied in Damascus, then pursued a doctorate in Islamic studies in Cairo, where he absorbed the teachings of Qutb. After several years teaching at Saudi Arabia's King Abdul Aziz University, in 1980 Azzam transferred to the newly opened International Islamic University that Saudi Arabia had funded in the Pakistani capital of Islamabad. After he moved to Peshawar, near the Afghan border, he oversaw the Maktab al-Khadamat (Services Office), which channeled thousands of Arab fighters into Afghanistan, and published his glossy full-color monthly magazine *al-Jihad*. Azzam also traveled worldwide (not least in the United States), raising political, financial, and logistical support for the jihad. One of the many young men he recruited was Osama bin Laden (1957–2011). After the two men disagreed about the strategy of the jihad, the younger and more militant bin Laden set up his own training camp to bypass Azzam's Maktab al-Khadamat. He called it simply al-Qaeda (the base).

However, the war in Afghanistan would not remain a regional affair for two reasons. The first was that it directly exposed thousands of young men from the Middle East, South Asia, and even Europe to the practical business of organizing jihad. The second was that the sheer volume of multilingual propaganda produced in Arabic, Urdu, Pashto, Persian, English, and many other languages spread the new interpretation of jihad far beyond those direct participants through magazines such as *al-Jihad* and *al-Mujahid* (Holy Warrior). Among the most influential of such jihad-inspiring writings was Azzam's spiritual memoir, *Ayat al-Rahman fi Jihad al-Afghan* (Signs of the Merciful God in the Afghan Jihad). As proof that the war was in line with God's will, Azzam described dozens of battlefield miracles that enabled humble Muslim warriors to defeat the Soviet goliath. First published in Arabic in Lahore, in 1984, other editions followed from Jeddah, Amman, Beirut, and Alexandria, after which it was translated into languages as varied as English, Urdu, Turkish, and Bahasa-Indonesia.

Through its funding, recruitment, organization, and textual production, the sheer internationalism of the Afghan jihad served to disseminate widely the revolutionary strand of global Islam first conceptualized by al-Banna, Maududi, and Qutb. Moreover, when the Soviets finally withdrew in 1989, the lesson was clearly that jihad worked as a strategy for defeating even the mightiest opponents.

Aside from transforming Afghanistan into a zone of permanent (and, since 1989, internecine) jihad, this transnational flow of texts, funds, and weapons would also reshape Islam in Pakistan. One reason for this was the policies of General Muhammad Zia-ul-Haq, who used his autocratic presidency of Pakistan from 1978 till his mysterious death a decade later to create a more Sharia-based Islamic state out of what had been founded in 1947 as a secular state for Muslims. While General Zia's transformative project remained incomplete—owing not least to the courage of the secular judiciary and civil society—it massively increased the role of Islam in Pakistani state policy, whether by promoting jihad in Afghanistan and Kashmir or by providing state funds for *madrasa* seminaries (many of which were also funded by Saudi Arabia). By the time of General Zia's death in 1988, Pakistan had acquired over 8,000 official *madrasas* and around 25,000 unofficial ones, compared with a total of around 900 in 1971.

The overall majority of these *madrasas* were aligned to the Deobandi movement, which was now expanding its influence beyond the Indo-Pakistani diaspora into Afghanistan and subsequently, as the Soviet Union collapsed, into central Asia. Jihadist breakaway adaptations of both Salafi and Deobandi Islam were moving into new world regions.

From antisocialist jihad to anti-imperialist revolution

The Soviet invasion of Afghanistan was only one of the seismic geopolitical shifts in 1979 that would transform the landscape of global Islam. The other was the Iranian Revolution, which ushered in a distinctively Shi'i form of Islamic state based on a novel hybrid of Shi'i doctrines and the radical Sunni teachings of Qutb and Maududi.

Since its ideological conception, the Iranian Revolution has had many transnational ties, whether through the Iraqi exile of its religious leader, Ayatullah Khomeini (1902–89), or through the Parisian years that taught its secular theorist Ali Shariati

(1933–77) to blend Marxism into a "Red Shi'ism" for the oppressed masses. In the lead-up to the revolution, new technologies dispersed such ideas through the smuggling of sermons on tape cassettes and subsequently through radio and television interviews. But it was not only Shariati who adapted political ideas from the Western spectrum of antidemocratic theories to justify the cause of revolution. Maududi borrowed his model of a revolutionary vanguard from Lenin, while Qutb absorbed the French eugenicist Alexis Carrel's critique of Europe's degenerate materialism. As noted earlier, their novel ideas in turn spread to Iran through Persian translations that influenced Khomeini's cadre of revolutionary clerics. Like Saudi Salafi-Wahhabism, the resulting political Shi'ism was a modern invention that overturned centuries of tradition.

Many tropes were borrowed from the ubiquitous communist discourse of the oppressed masses. Islamic revolutionaries were, after all, competing with the communists, who had many followers among the Iranian (as well as the Pakistani and Afghan) intelligentsia. But rising above the monotonous repetition of these familiar slogans came Khomeini's call to implement an alternative type of politics based around the new political theology of *vilayat-i faqih* (rule of the jurisconsult). In the name of liberation from imperialism—now American, not European—this would effectively centralize state power around a single Shi'i interpreter of Sharia. That interpreter was Khomeini himself.

After the Islamic Republic of Iran was established in April 1979, the new Iranian constitution declared Khomeini the Rahbar-i Mu'azzam (Supreme Leader) not just of Shi'i Iranians, but of all Muslims worldwide. It was a claim of authority that Khomeini repeatedly reiterated in his speeches over the next decade. His revolutionary Shi'ism was exported with generous state support, albeit with increasing pushback from Saudi Arabia and Bahrain, who worried about their own marginalized Shi'i populations.

As Iran competed with Saudi Arabia for international influence, political Islam became a mechanism for Iranian—and Shi'i— power projection via foreign policy. Responding to the Saudi Islamic University of Madinah, in 1979 one of the earliest acts of the Islamic Republic of Iran was to establish Jami'at al-Mustafa al-'Alamiya (al-Mustafa International University) in Qom, followed by the Imam Khomeini University of Islamic Sciences and the Madrasa al-Hujjatiyya. Together they would introduce Khomeini's politicized Shi'ism to students recruited with scholarships from the minority Shi'i populations of South Asia, Lebanon, the Gulf states, Syria, Azerbaijan, Tajikistan, and elsewhere. After the Iranian embassy sponsored the construction of a Shi'i mosque in Buenos Aires in 1983, its second imam was an Argentinian graduate of Imam Khomeini University. Meanwhile, like its Saudi Sunni rival, al-Mustafa International University emphasized the importance of *tabligh* (propagation). Over the following years, its graduates founded branches in sixty other countries. When Indonesian graduates of al-Mustafa returned home to establish their own Islamic College in Jakarta, this new form of missionary Shi'ism even breached the historically Sunni watershed of maritime Southeast Asia.

Exporting revolution was not only a matter of education. After Tehran's Office of Liberation Movements was set up in 1981, as the Marxist notion of imperialist oppression was Islamized through allegories of the early Shi'i martyrs, attempts were also made to create militant organizations to empower "oppressed" Shi'is in other countries. The most influential result came in Lebanon through the founding of Hizbullah (Party of Allah) in 1985, though two years earlier Saudi Shi'is studying in Qom had founded their own Saudi Arabian franchise, Hizbullah al-Hijaz.

Another opportunity for Iran to spread its revolutionary religiosity came through the war in neighboring Afghanistan, where the downtrodden ethnic group of the Hazaras constituted a large Shi'i minority. Iranian officials viewed the Hazaras as a means of countering Saudi influence in their backyard. As up to 2.8 million Afghans sought refuge in Iran, scholarships were offered to cultivate among the Hazaras a new generation of politicized religious leaders. Such Iran-educated Hazaras would subsequently transform Afghan Shi'ism, albeit without necessarily toeing a pro-Iranian line. The same held true in neighboring Pakistan, whose Shi'i minority was being marginalized by the Sunni Islamizing policies of General Zia. Elsewhere, Iranian cultural centers were attached to embassies to distribute polished translations of Shi'i political and theological texts.

As a Shi'i counterweight to Saudi Arabia, Iran showed how autocratic Islamic states could monopolize resources (especially oil revenues) to promote a particular version of Islam far beyond its national borders. In Saudi Arabia, Pakistan, and then Iran, the rise of the state as a religious actor marked a new stage in the development of global Islam and the competition to control it.

Transnational responses of traditionalist Shi'ism

Despite its many attempts, the Islamic Republic of Iran was unable to monopolize the Shi'i input into global Islam. As a counterweight, nonstate Shi'i activists and organizations found other opportunities through globalization to reject such state initiatives.

In the 1980s, traditionalist Shi'i *ulama* who opposed Khomeini's political theology emigrated from Iran and Iraq to the Damascus suburb of Sayyida Zaynab, where they established alternatives to the state seminaries of Qom. Other clerical exiles founded organizations elsewhere. The largest of these new nonpolitical Twelver Shi'i organizations was the Al-Khoei Benevolent Foundation, established by Ayatullah Abu al-Qasim al-Khu'i (1889–1992), a theological moderate and skilled administrator of large religious endowments. After its headquarters moved to London in 1989 at the height of Saddam Hussein's persecution of Iraqi Shi'is, Al-Khoei went on to found another fifteen international branches, as well as to undertake charitable activities aimed at ameliorating the condition of Shi'i minorities worldwide.

In an entirely new geographical move, traditionalist Shi'ism was also by now entering Africa via preachers from India and Lebanon. This development was first initiated by the Indian Sa'id Akhtar Rizvi (1927–2002), who in 1964 established the Bilal Muslim Mission to counter the spread of Sunnism and Christianity. Named after the Prophet's Ethiopian follower, it founded schools and published a magazine in Swahili called *Sauti ya Bilal* (Voice of Bilal), eventually expanding inland from Tanzania into Rwanda and what was then Zaire. By the early 1980s, the Iraqi-trained Lebanese missionary Abd al-Mun'am al-Zayn (b. 1945) was also converting hundreds of West Africans to Shi'ism via preaching tours through Côte d'Ivoire, Guinea Conakry, Gambia, Guinea-Bissau, and Sierra Leone. Even so, after West African students were sponsored to study in Shi'i seminaries in Iran, some did begin to espouse political Shi'ism. The most prominent of these African students was Ibrahim El-Zakzaky (b. 1953), whose Islamic Movement of Nigeria began a campaign for Islamic government and stricter observance of Sharia.

By the 1990s, individual activists, transnational organizations, and the Islamic Republic of Iran were competing worldwide to control the teachings of Shi'i Islam.

An Islamic scramble for Africa

Africa had also become a major focus of Saudi attention, not least through policies that viewed education in terms of community empowerment. In much of Africa, Muslims had fewer educational opportunities, and subsequently less sociopolitical influence, than local Christians, who had benefited from the missionary schools founded in the colonial period. In response, the Islamic University in Niger opened in 1986, and the Islamic University in Uganda enrolled its first students two years later. Graduates of the Islamic University of Madinah were sent by Saudi state agencies to more than twenty different African countries. Between 1982 and 1997, the highest participation rate in the *dawrat* (proselytizing tours) conducted by the Islamic University of Madinah came from Nigeria, which sent over 8,000 students.

As in other regions of the world, Saudi global outreach generated local responses in Nigeria, such as the Jama'at Izalat al-Bid'a wa Iqamat al-Sunna (Society for the Removal of Innovation and the Reestablishment of the Sunna). Along with distributing Salafi-Wahhabi textbooks, its members sought to undermine the often hereditary and wealthy Sufi leaders who represented world Islam in West Africa. By now, the multidirectional Salafi outreach to Africa was acquiring its own dynamics, not least as the return of graduates from the various Islamic universities generated competition for leadership. One example is the Islamic University of Madinah graduate Ja'far Mahmud Adam (1960–2007), who founded the Ahlussunnah (People of the Sunna) in the Nigerian city of Kano as a challenge to the Izala Society, whose leaders, Adam claimed, were insufficiently versed in Salafi writings. Other disagreements emerged through attempts to interpret Salafism in ways that were most meaningful or effective in different African settings. Many of these intra-Salafi debates concerned the question of whether local Sufis should be condemned as non-Muslims and the extent to which Salafis should engage with politicians in the push to implement Sharia. There was also much disagreement on the permissibility of violence.

African associates of Saudi Arabia acted as local intermediaries. One such Salafi middleman was the Nigerian Abubakr Gumi (1924–92), who in addition to many African preaching tours published tracts undermining Africa's Sufi traditions and in 1979 translated the Quran into Hausa under Saudi sponsorship. As access to television expanded, Gumi took to debating Sufis on programs watched by large audiences intrigued by the novelty of public challenges to wealthy leaders of Nigeria's long-standing Sufi establishment. These activities won him the King Faisal Award for Services to Islam. Similar developments were occurring across Africa: returnee students, with the prestige of Saudi diplomas and fluent Arabic, positioned themselves as new religious authorities who transmitted the pure Islam of Mecca rather than what they condemned as the superstitions of local Sufis.

Similar developments were also at work in other West African countries, such as Ghana, where Salafi ideas had earlier been introduced by Yusuf Soalih (also known as Afa Ajura, d. 2004) through the Anbariya Islamic Institute he established in the city of Tamale. Ghana subsequently gained a considerable cadre of returnee graduates from Saudi Arabia, their influence bolstered by the high prestige of studies in Mecca or Medina. As in Nigeria, these graduates founded their own organizations in turn, which increasingly took the acceptable guise of NGOs, a term domesticated via the Arabic term *ghayr hukumiyya* alongside the older religious term for charity, *khayriyya*.

As with the emergence of the first Muslim missionary organizations half a century earlier, in the 1980s concerns that Christian charities were either winning converts or discriminating against Muslims generated a massive growth of Islamic NGOs across Africa. Many of Africa's new Islamic NGOs received their funding from the Gulf states, as in the case of Saudi Arabia's International Islamic Relief Organization (founded in 1978) and Kuwait's Africa Muslims Agency (founded in 1981). As the decade progressed, the global television news publicity that attended African humanitarian crises brought other new Islamic NGOs to the continent. By defining themselves as nonpolitical aid agencies, some Islamic charities adopted the influential Salafi Nasir al-Din al-Albani's conception of *da'wa* (propagation) as a practical business of building mosques, schools, and hospitals. Although these Islamic NGOs did not promote violence—many employees and volunteers were doctors and teachers—they did help institutionalize Salafism in the interior of Africa, where the traditional religious establishments of world Islam had previously been unchallenged.

Via a network of Saudi-affiliated NGOs, universities, institutes, and think tanks that sought to define Islam for governments and publics alike, the 1980s saw Saudi Arabia's role as a religious exporter influence an extraordinary number of places.

Competing Pakistani preaching societies

Despite the vast resources lent by Saudi oil revenue, the self-funded missionaries of the Tablighi Jamaat (founded in India in 1927) developed a remarkably effective model of grassroots evangelicalism. But their adherence to a stripped-down, anti-Sufi version of Deobandi theology also prompted competition from Pakistani preachers who sought to defend the devotional rituals of South Asia's traditional Sufi Islam.

The Tablighi Jamaat mainly expanded from Pakistan by means of its trademark dozen-strong voluntary *jama'ats*. But beginning in the 1970s, institutional bases emerged in various other countries, as Indonesian cities such as Solo became major regional hubs for the Tablighi outreach across Southeast Asia. In 1972, a French franchise, Foi et Practique (Faith and Practice), was founded in Paris, followed in 1975 by its first formal organizations in Belgium and Morocco. Then, in 1980, the Dar al-Ulum Islamic Institute was set up in the northern English town of Dewsbury, which would subsequently serve as the Tablighi Jamaat's proselytizing headquarters in Europe.

While the Tablighi Jamaat served as the main mechanism for the spread of Sharia-oriented but nonpolitical Deobandi Islam, its lay-preacher model was complemented by the founding of seminaries tasked with training more educated *ulama*. Aside from the hundreds of Deobandi *madrasas* established in Pakistan and Bangladesh, in 1971 the Jamia Dar al-Ulum was established in the Iranian city of Zahedan, enabling Deobandi ideas to spread among the large Sunni minority in Iran. In 1973, three other *madrasas* opened in Newcastle, South Africa, and the British cities of Bury and Birmingham, promoting the careful study of traditional texts and even sometimes mystical practices. In 1986, America's first Deobandi seminary opened in Buffalo, New York.

By way of opposition, seminaries were founded in Britain, North America, and South Africa by *ulama* affiliated with Barelvi theology. Barelvism had emerged in the early 1900s to defend from Deobandi polemics the popular shrine rituals through which millions of South Asian Muslims expressed their devotion to the Sufi saints and the Prophet. However, this competing outreach to the same regions led to the export of Barelvi–Deobandi disputes between mosques and *madrasas* under their respective control in places as far apart as Durban and Birmingham. But while the Deobandi ties to the Tablighi Jamaat helped spread their Islam beyond their original South Asian heritage audience, the strong Barelvi ties to distinctly South Asian devotional practices limited their wider global appeal.

In 1981, Barelvi opponents to the Deobandi-linked Tablighi Jamaat launched a countermission called Dawat-e-Islami (Islamic Propagation). Its founder was a Pakistani businessman called Muhammad Ilyas Qadiri Attar (b. 1950). Dawat-e-Islami began by copying the low-cost Tablighi methods, encouraging members to join small *madani qafila* (missionary caravans) and ask people to complete spiritual self-assessment forms called *madani inamat*. However, as membership and revenues grew, mirroring the Deobandi strategy, Dawat-e-Islami began building a series of seminaries called Jamiat-ul-Madina (Medina Universities) in Africa, Britain, and elsewhere.

In 2008, Dawat-e-Islami launched a satellite television channel called Madani TV, with programming in English, Urdu, and Bangla and plans for further expansion into Arabic to spread Barelvi doctrines to the Gulf. But by then, a fragmenting digital spectrum of rival Muslim satellite channels was already visible to viewers worldwide.

The many forms of Muslim Brotherhood

The decades after 1970 also saw the politically oriented Muslim Brotherhood splinter into competing but nonetheless increasingly influential factions. Both wings, the violent and nonviolent, found new areas of activity.

After Anwar Sadat became president of Egypt in 1970, imprisoned members of the Brotherhood were gradually released, and its social welfare activities were tolerated, even though the organization remained technically illegal. By then, its years of persecution in Egypt had led exiled members to build an extensive overseas network, which was expanding in Europe and North America. The move to the Muslim-minority environments of Europe caused both the Brotherhood and other Salafis to generate an important new theological concept that would underpin their activities there. Rather than the medieval legal dichotomy of a *dar al-Islam* (region of Islam) and *dar al-harb* (region of war), which divided the world into zones that were ruled by Muslims and those that were not, influential Salafi thinkers such as Yusuf al-Qaradawi (1926–) presented Europe as a new kind of legal space: the *dar al-da'wa* (region of propagation).

With no old and established Islamic religious authorities of the kind that existed in long-standing Muslim regions, this third space offered the Brotherhood's many offshoot organizations something approaching a religiously blank slate on which, through propagation of many kinds, they could try to define Islam on their own terms. In its new European environments, the Brotherhood took on a variety of locally legitimate forms, such as community and civil rights groups, that were both functionally and financially independent from Cairo. Thus, as it expanded, the Brotherhood became not a single organization but a global federation of many regional, national, and local organizations. Even so, it is also worth pointing out where the Brotherhood was not able to establish itself, namely the Soviet Union and China, despite the fact that both regions were home to far more Muslims than western Europe.

Meanwhile, the rapprochement with President Sadat saw the Cairo leadership of the Egyptian Brotherhood officially renounce violence. This led one faction of the Brotherhood to focus on education rather than revolution as the means to achieve its founder's goal of creating a Sharia-based sociopolitical order. This gradualist strategy, which also made its way to Europe, involved either founding or gaining influence over educational institutions. But another faction of the Brotherhood was inspired by the revolutionary Sayyid Qutb, editions and translations of whose works proliferated after his martyr's execution in 1966. As we have seen, the anti-Soviet war in Afghanistan provided Qutb's followers with an opportunity to put his revolutionary jihadist ideas into practice.

By the 1990s, the Brotherhood's version of Salafism had taken on various contradictory forms as its increasing number of representatives negotiated diverse political environments from the Middle East to Afghanistan, Africa and Europe.

Rival relocations to Europe

The intensification of globalization during the 1990s generated more complex, multidirectional religious transfers than in previous decades, when regions such as Europe and Africa were largely reception zones for global Islamic organizations. In the late twentieth century, both continents became Muslim religious exporters as well as importers, with the United States also starting to play this role.

Crucial to this development was the role played by European cities as enclaves for transnational Islamic religious organizations, which in some cases outmaneuvered attempts by European-born Muslims to promote their own institutions. Many factors contributed to this relocation. Western European nations offered much greater freedoms of religion and speech than many Muslim-majority countries; furthermore, major European cities were global transportation hubs. The strategy of relocation was pioneered by the Muslim Brotherhood, after it reestablished itself in Munich and then other European cities to escape persecution in Egypt. The strategy became even more important after the Brotherhood was brutally suppressed in Syria, having seized control of the city of Hama in 1982. Other Islamic political organizations followed it into the greater freedoms of European exile. One was Millî Görüş (National Vision, founded 1969), which relocated from Turkey to Germany in the 1980s after falling under the scrutiny of what was then stridently secular Turkish officialdom.

In 1984, persecution of a different kind led the Pakistani heirs of the nineteenth-century Indian Muslim messiah Mirza Ghulam Ahmad to relocate their headquarters to London. The trigger was the anti-Ahmadiyya Ordinance XX, issued by Pakistan's Sunni president, General Zia. The law effectively declared the Ahmadiyya to be non-Muslims, banning them not only from preaching but also from professing their beliefs in their homeland. As the earliest global Muslim missionary organization, the Ahmadiyya sought to maintain this program from London, sending low-key missions and founding Ahmadi mosques in cities as far apart as Manila (1985), Bangkok (1986), and Guatemala City (1989). They also achieved some success in West Africa, particularly in Benin, Ghana, and Gambia. But despite the freedoms of exile, the Ahmadiyya were less successful in the Middle East and South Asia, where Salafis and Deobandis loudly denounced them as apostates.

The lingering imperial networks that had brought the Ahmadiyya to London and aided its Anglophone outreach to places such as Ghana also enabled quite different organizations of South Asian origin to expand into Africa via Britain. One example was the Islamic Foundation, founded in 1973 by Pakistani supporters of Maududi in the factory town of Leicester before acquiring a large complex in nearby rural Markfield in 1990. By then, its founder, Khurshid Ahmad (1932–), had gained state support as a Pakistani government minister tasked by General Zia with Islamizing the economy. Via Karachi and Markfield, the Islamic Foundation established branches in Lagos and Nairobi (albeit with South Asian rather than African directors), which in turn founded Mombasa's Kisauni Islamic University.

Half a century after Anglophone Ahmadiyya missionaries from India began converting African Americans in Detroit and Chicago, African American organizations began their own outreach overseas via the Nation of Islam, founded in Detroit back in 1930. When Warith Deen Mohammed (1933–2008) became leader in 1975, he sent representatives to Belize, Trinidad, Guyana, and Jamaica, as well as Britain. After disbanding the Nation of Islam, he founded the American Society of Muslims and imitated the international preaching of Malcolm X (1925–65), who had toured Africa and Europe after his break with the Nation. While Mohammed downplayed the movement's earlier emphasis on African American empowerment (and even supremacy), these ideas were revived when the Nation was re-established in 1981. Such doctrines inevitably limited its wider appeal, seeing the Nation's outreach deliberately confined to the African diaspora. Nonetheless, this marked a moment when America was becoming an exporter of its own particularist Islam, even as Malcolm X and

Warith Deen Mohammed denounced the Nation of Islam in favor of more universalist forms of religiosity.

Meanwhile, the Iranian Revolution inadvertently led to the founding of small-scale Sufi organizations in Europe by exiles such as Javad Nurbakhsh (1926–2008). After fleeing Iran, he founded branches of his Khaniqah Nimatullahi brotherhood in Britain, the United States, and the Netherlands, while self-publishing many books (mainly in English). Utilizing his degree in psychology from the Sorbonne, Nurbakhsh reinterpreted medieval Persian Sufi texts via Western psychology. Another Sufi exile organization was the Naqshbandi Haqqani Sufi Order, led by the Turkish Cypriot Nazim al-Haqqani (1922–2014). After first visiting London in 1974, the 1980s and '90s saw him gain small groups of followers across western Europe and the United States.

Nonetheless, when the Brussels-based Federation of Islamic Organizations in Europe was established in 1989, followed by the Dublin-based European Council for Fatwa and Research, their members were not Sufis, but influential Salafis such as the Egyptian Yusuf al-Qaradawi. Founded to define the contours of Islam in Europe, with the appearance of democratic councils and think tanks, such organizations presented Salafism to European policy-makers as normative Islam.

Many smaller European Muslim organizations became more ethical than political in orientation, conceiving the West as a 'space of testimony' (*dar al-shahada*). Far from promoting violence, they merely sought to protect Europe's growing Muslim-heritage populations from the moral void of materialism.

Africa as a global exporter of Islam

Since the 1980s, African cities had been joining their European counterparts in becoming hubs from which global Islamic organizations emanated as well as entered, albeit not necessarily under African leadership.

A case in point is the Islamic Propagation Centre International, founded in 1980 by Ahmed Deedat (1918–2005), a former businessman born in India. Based in Durban, South Africa, Deedat initially used his organization to distribute Salafi-Wahhabi texts. But after debating the Pentecostal televangelist Jimmy Swaggart on a preaching tour of the United States, he adopted the mass-media approach of American evangelical Christians. As videocassette players caught on, his South African Propagation Center supplied tapes of his debates with non-Muslims to audiences on both sides of the Indian Ocean, as well as Britain and America.

The combined role of South Asians in Africa and English as a global language also helped the Tablighi Jamaat expand further across Africa, increasingly through the efforts of Africans themselves. By 1986, Nigerian preachers had spread the Tablighi Jamaat into Benin, with two large Tablighi centers soon following in the Mauritanian capital, Nouakchott. As socialist policies withered with the collapse of the Soviet Union, similar inter-African dynamics aided the expansion of the Muslim Brotherhood. Amid the political reforms of postsocialist Ethiopia, in 1991 the Somali branch of the Muslim Brotherhood established a franchise called Tadamun (Solidarity) for the marginalized Muslim minority in neighboring Ethiopia.

However, the most significant factor in the spread of political Islam through Africa's Sahel region came via the formation of an Islamic state in Sudan. This was largely the creation of Hassan al-Turabi (1932–2016), who, after studying to the doctoral level in London and Paris, gained prominence through the Muslim Brotherhood–modeled National Islamic Front, which he founded on his return to Khartoum. After encouraging President Jaafar Nimeiri (1928–2009) to institutionalize Sharia in 1983, when

General Omar al-Bashir led a military coup in 1989, Turabi became the power behind the throne. He went on to implement state policies that transformed Sudan into an African promoter of political Islam.

In 1991, Turabi masterminded the Popular Arab Islamic Conference, which brought to Khartoum around 500 representatives of Islamic political organizations from forty different countries. They included delegates from the Islamic Republic of Iran, the Jordanian Muslim Brotherhood, Palestine's recently founded Hamas, and *mujahidin* leaders from Afghanistan. One outcome of the conference was the relocation to Sudan of Osama bin Laden and his nascent organization al-Qaeda, which remained there till 1996. Using Sudanese oil revenues, Turabi founded the African Islamic University in Khartoum to rear a new generation of political Islamic activists across Africa. Yet the university taught secular as well as religious subjects, sponsoring impoverished students from as far away as Afghanistan to study medicine. Turabi also began sending Islamic NGOs to spread both his political vision and developmental aid to other regions of the continent.

However, the 1980s also saw several African Sufi organizations export their nonpolitical religious vision outside their home regions. During the second half of the twentieth century, the shrine of Amadou Bamba (1853–1927), in the Senegalese city of Touba (Repentance), became an important destination of Sufi pilgrims for his increasingly widespread African followers, called Mourides (Seekers). Via the West African small-trader diaspora, they subsequently expanded to Europe and the United States. Establishing their distinctive *da'iras* (teaching circles) in cities including Marseilles and New York, the Mourides gained new followers, particularly among migrants from Africa.

Similarly, an energetic offshoot of the Tijaniyya Sufi brotherhood founded by Ibrahim Niasse (1900–1975) gained support outside

9. As Africa shifted from being an importer to an exporter of global Islam, a few of its Sufi brotherhoods found followers among the African diaspora. Anchored to their Senegalese center, Mourides go on pilgrimage to the shrine of Amadou Bamba in Touba.

his native Senegal. Initially this came through Niasse's tours of West Africa, on which he often preached to crowds of thousands, but in the years after his death, Wolof and Arabic cassette recordings of his sermons won followers across North Africa. So did the preaching circuits of his son, Hassan Cisse (1945–2008), who toured North America, the Caribbean, and Malaysia, and his grandson, Tidiane Ali Cisse (1955–), who gained convert followers among the African diaspora in Europe.

By the start of the new millennium, emissaries of Africa's rich Islamic heritage were making a limited but increasing contribution to the beleaguered Sufi current of global Islam.

The opening up of China

Having been effectively closed for decades, China saw even more dramatic religious changes than Africa and Europe. Under Deng

Xiaoping, the Communist Party of China's new economic policy of "reform and opening up" during the 1980s lifted restrictions on Muslim worship, mosque building, and pilgrimage.

Partly in an attempt to win the economic support of wealthy countries in the Gulf, between 1980 and 1987 China hosted thirty-six religious delegations from twenty Islamic countries, allowed more than 2,000 Chinese Muslims to make the *hajj*, and funded others to undertake religious studies in Egypt and Pakistan. The Saudi response was to give hundreds of Chinese students scholarships for the Islamic University of Madinah. Moving in the opposite direction, preachers and teachers were dispatched to China from Saudi Arabia under the auspices of the Muslim World League, which also funded the construction and renovation of Chinese mosques. Compared to China's traditional mosques, which mirrored the architecture of Sino-Buddhist temples, the new mosques were built in the plainer form favored in the Gulf.

While Saudi-influenced Chinese promotors of Salafism were a small minority among China's approximately 25 million Muslim-heritage citizens, they gained influence through their impact on the state-sanctioned Islamic Association of China. As in other regions, these largely nonpolitical Salafis condemned the older world Islam that had slowly evolved among the Hui. A particular focus of critique was the traditional *jingtang jiaoyu* (scripture-hall education), which incorporated Chinese translations of medieval Persian Sufi classics. Instead, wealthy Saudi religious charities deployed donated Qurans as vehicles of influence through translations, commentaries, and appendices that promoted a Salafi-Wahhabi reading of scripture. In 1987 alone, over a million such Qurans were distributed across China, a gift from King Fahd, as part of the great Saudi pushback against godless communism.

Meanwhile, the Tablighi Jamaat also reached China, with its first party of nonpolitical lay preachers arriving from Malegaon, India, in 1986. A decade later, its missionaries were operating in Xining, the heartland of the ethnic Chinese Hui Muslims.

Having made use of China's open borders, Tablighi and Salafi preachers were soon competing for the loyalty of the Hui in the formerly remote province of Qinghai, on the highland borders of Tibet.

The opening up of post-Soviet central Asia

However, it was central Asia that became global Islam's newest frontier. In December 1991, the dissolution of the Soviet Union suddenly opened the borders of a series of new nation-states whose Muslim-heritage populations had been exposed to seventy years of socialist de-Islamization policies.

A flurry of competing Islamic organizations rapidly mobilized to re-Islamize the region. While some were state-sponsored, the majority were nonstate entities. Many came in the guise of the Islamic NGOs and charities that had proliferated over the previous decade, offering to supply schools, mosques, and religious texts that were banned in Soviet times. In contrast to the nineteenth-century role of the Russian Empire in exporting the modernist Jadid movement and central Asia's older history of disseminating Naqshbandi Sufism, the post-Soviet sphere now became an even greater religious importer than China.

Among the earliest to arrive was the Pakistan-based Tablighi Jamaat. Its lay preachers by now had experience of almost every corner of the globe and had already established underground circles in central Asia via Soviet student-exchange programs with the developing world. The low-cost operations of the Tablighis were soon at work among the newly independent citizens of Uzbekistan, Kazakhstan, Turkmenistan, and especially Tajikistan and Kyrgyzstan. But their various competitors also promptly appeared on the scene, including the messianic, nonpolitical

Ahmadiyya, by now based in London, who in 1991 established their first post-Soviet outpost in Kazakhstan. Canada- and UK-based Shi'i Ismailis soon followed via the Aga Khan Development Network, which formed ties with the Ismaili-heritage inhabitants of highland Tajikistan. It also offered health and educational facilities to the broader population through such projects as the University of Central Asia, formally established in 2000.

Ethnolinguistic affinities encouraged various Turkish organizations to reach out to central Asia. Several were followers of the nonpolitical modernist-*cum*-mystic Sa'id Nursi (1876–1960), particularly the Hizmet Hareketi (Service Movement) founded by Fethullah Gülen (b. 1941) and named after Nursi's concept of *hizmet-i imaniye ve Kur'aniye* (service to the faith and the Quran). Despite using the appealing language of Sufism in books aimed at Western readers, in central Asia Gülen substantially rejected many traditional mystical practices in favor of the social activism emphasized in his organization's name. At the same time that it was expanding through Europe and North America via donations from Turkey's flourishing industrialists, Gülen's Hizmet founded scores of modern schools across central Asia. Mirroring albeit competing with Salafi outreach strategies, Hizmet fostered a post-Soviet Muslim elite that for several years included the chief advisor to the president of Turkmenistan.

Far from standing by, the Turkish state became an even more significant religious actor. Its Diyanet İşleri Başkanlığı (Directorate of Religious Affairs) sent hundreds of imams to central Asia, funded Sovietized students to study in Turkey's state-approved seminaries, and published religious primers in central Asian languages. After the prime minister of Turkey, Turgut Özal (1927–93), himself a Sufi follower of the Naqshbandi-Khalidi brotherhood, contributed state funds to restore the neglected shrines of Uzbekistan's Naqshbandis, the Sufi brotherhoods crept out of the secular shadows of Turkish republicanism to seek new followers in the region. One such Turkish Sufi leader was Osman

Nuri Topbaş (b. 1942), whose books for the postcommunist public were translated into Albanian, Kazakh, and Azeri.

Not to be outmaneuvered in its backyard, the Islamic Republic of Iran organized its own religious outreach to central Asia. Shi'i Iran tackled the denominational obstacle of influencing a historically Sunni population by delegating the task to the state-sanctioned Sunni organizations its government permitted to operate among Iran's own Sunni minorities. As a result, the Deobandi *madrasas* that opened in Iranian Baluchistan during the 1970s served as Iran's unlikely proxies.

Representatives of a more transparently political Islam were also among the entrants to central Asia's new religious marketplace. The most effective was Hizb al-Tahrir al-Islamiya (Islamic Liberation Party), founded in East Jerusalem in 1953 with the ambition of establishing a transnational caliphate. During the 1990s, while gaining a foothold on university campuses in Britain, Hizb al-Tahrir expanded into Tajikistan, Uzbekistan, Kazakhstan, and Kyrgyzstan, recruiting thousands of members in each country. It was only one of several transnational militant organizations that entered the political vacuum left by the collapse of communism. Violent insurrections followed. The largest was the civil war in Tajikistan from 1992 to 1997, which saw the Islamic Renaissance Party of Tajikistan (Hizb-i Nahzat-i Islami-yi Tajikistan) fighting to found an Islamic state with help from more experienced transnational mujahidin from Afghanistan.

Watching with horror, central Asia's nascent nationalist governments did not allow the region's chaotically globalized religious marketplace to remain unregulated for much longer. First Kazakhstan, then Uzbekistan and Turkmenistan began closing their borders to many global Islamic organizations. In 2000, this nationalist pushback even saw Gülen's purportedly nonpolitical Hizmet expelled from Uzbekistan and its schools closed, with Turkmenistan following suit in 2011, Tajikistan four years later, and then Azerbaijan in 2016 (though Hizmet schools remained open in Kyrgyzstan). While this was partly the result of pressure from the Turkish government, the closures also marked the revival of Soviet statist religious policies.

Despite having a far larger Muslim population than any other European state, post-Soviet Russia opened its borders to few if any global Islamic organizations, particularly after its brutal suppression of the independence movement in its satellite state of Chechnya, which drew in small brigades of foreign jihadists. After their initial period of open experimentation, central Asia's secular autocracies increasingly followed Russia's lead.

The "little jihads" of the 1990s

The wars in Chechnya and Tajikistan belonged to the series of "little jihads" that spread throughout the 1990s through the transfer of ideas, personnel, or organizations from Afghanistan and the proliferation of Sayyid Qutb's violent version of Salafism.

These conflicts were little only in comparison to the geopolitical magnitude of the Afghan jihad: in Algeria alone, the war between the secular nationalist government and the Front Islamique du Salut (Islamic Salvation Front) resulted in somewhere between 44,000 and 150,000 deaths. Often taking advantage of conflicts connected to the end of the Cold War, in the course of the 1990s other transnational jihad groups established themselves amid civil disorder or outright war in Bosnia, Chechnya, Somalia, and Yemen, as well as Kashmir. Meanwhile, the war in Afghanistan continued among rival factions of mujahidin with different political visions. These local conflicts drew in international participants, some with financial support from Saudi Arabia and Pakistan.

The collective scale of these conflicts caused a massive transnational redistribution of the propaganda, personnel, and practical expertise that had first crystallized around the anti-Soviet struggle in Afghanistan. By passing the ideology and methods of the little jihads to new generations elsewhere, this in turn helped inspire third-wave jihads in other regions where Muslims felt marginalized, such as the southern Philippines and the African Sahel.

Few of these violent strategies of religious coercion were successful in reaching their end goal of setting up Islamic states of the kind theorized by al-Banna, Maududi, and Qutb a few decades earlier. But the 1990s did see some new Islamic states emerge from these struggles, the earliest being the short-lived Salafi Emirate of Kunar, founded in 1990 in Afghanistan by Jamil al-Rahman (1939–91) and his Jama'at al Da'wa al-Quran (Society for the Call to the Quran). By 1996, the younger Taliban heirs to the mujahidin of the 1980s had succeeded in establishing their larger Islamic Emirate of Afghanistan.

As implied by the name Taliban (Students), the early recruits were former *madrasa* students. Many of their leaders were graduates of a single *madrasa*: the Dar al-Ulum Haqqaniya in the small Pakistani border town of Akora Khattak. Despite its backwater location, it bore the prestige of having been founded in 1947 by Abd al-Haq (1912–88), an esteemed graduate of the Deoband mother-*madrasa* in India. Initially, the youthful Taliban leadership used their network of fellow students and teachers to gain followers from the many makeshift *madrasas* set up in Pakistani refugee camps with funding and textbooks from Saudi Arabia. But after coming to power in Afghanistan, the Taliban subsequently widened their transnational ties through alliances with other militant organizations, most notably al-Qaeda.

Whether in terms of its organization, personnel, or political theology, al-Qaeda was a truly global enterprise, its activities stretching across Saudi Arabia, Yemen, Sudan, Kenya, Afghanistan, and Germany, before it attacked the United States in September 2001. The attack on the World Trade Center marked the moment when the post-Soviet jihads of the 1990s moved from the peripheries of the new neoliberal world order in places like Tajikistan and Chechnya to its center in New York. Shortly after 9/11, bin Laden explained his motives to audiences worldwide in a video cassette dispatched from rural Afghanistan to the satellite news channel Al Jazeera, recently established in Qatar.

The roots of bin Laden's revolutionary life lay in the years when Muslim Brotherhood members had traveled to Saudi Arabia, drawing bin Laden to study with Sayyid Qutb's brother, Muhammad Qutb (1919–2014), at King Abd al-Aziz University in bin Laden's hometown of Jeddah. But the Brotherhood's vision of Islamic statehood had always sat awkwardly with Saudi Arabia's official Salafi-Wahhabi doctrine of loyalty to the Saudi royal family. By the 1990s, Saudi Arabia began facing the unforeseen consequences of its collusion with the Brotherhood against the Arab nationalists. Promoted by several satellite television stations as well as universities and informal study circles, the Brotherhood's political Salafism generated not only al-Qaeda, which considered the Saudi state to be the primary enemy, but also the Sahwa al-Islamiyya (Islamic Awakening) movement, which opposed the Saudi dynasty on its home ground. In 1995 and again in 2003, a series of bombings in Riyadh were linked to the Sahwa.

Even so, Saudi Arabia continued to sponsor its unstable compound of Salafi-Wahhabism, not least in Southeast Asia via organizations such as the Dewan Dakwah Islamiyah Indonesia (Indonesian Council of Islamic Proselytizing). The Ihya al-Sunna *madrasa* opened in Yogyakarta in 1994, and the next five years saw more than a dozen other Salafi-Wahhabi *madrasas* established in Indonesia. While still a small minority compared to Indonesia's traditional *pesantren* seminaries, the new *madrasas* had curricula designed to train missionaries (*du'at*) in spreading their doctrines and undermining the region's ties to traditional world Islam. Yet as in Saudi Arabia itself, in Southeast Asia Salafi-Wahhabsm began transforming in ways that its original state sponsors were unable to control. Thus, when the Indonesian Jafar Umar Thalib (b. 1961) returned home from a long sojourn in Afghanistan, Pakistan, and Yemen, he set about preaching revolutionary jihadism via religious schools in Java.

Violence ensued, including the 2002 Bali bombings carried out by Jemaah Islamiyah (Islamic Society), a transnational Southeast Asian affiliate of al-Qaeda founded in 1993.

From nongovernmental organizations to Islamic banking

While such events caught the headlines, the last two decades of the twentieth century also saw the foundation of dozens of transnational charities. While some channeled funds to jihadists, most did not.

Pioneered by the Saudi-based International Islamic Relief Organization in 1978, this was a new organizational form of global Islam modeled on older Christian charities. Next came Islamic Relief Worldwide, founded in the British city of Birmingham in 1984 before acquiring field offices in twenty-five countries. Many other Islamic NGOs soon followed. As philanthropic expressions of religious solidarity, in the 1990s and 2000s these new Islamic charities evolved from two particular expressions of globalization. The first was cognitive: the increasing consciousness of Muslims from different world regions that they were members of a single community as the conceptual legacy of the Ottoman campaign for Islamic unity spread through the new global satellite tv and online media. The second was financial: the increasing ease of ransferring money across borders enabled by the financial deregulations of neoliberalism.

Some charities focused on *da'wa* (propagation) by building mosques and schools; some focused on the provision of medical and food aid. An undetermined number of others served as mechanisms of transmitting funds for political objectives. But all involved the movement across multiple borders of money, personnel, ideas, and institutions. As in other aspects of Islam's globalization, these flows between different regions were unequal, tending to pour out of the Gulf and Western diasporas into underdeveloped regions of Africa and war zones such as Bosnia and Afghanistan.

In addition to charities, another new institutional expression of global Islam emerged by way of Sharia-compliant banking that avoided interest as a forbidden form of *riba* (usury). In the 1990s, the deregulation of currency controls and the emergence of major European cities as global financial centers allowed many such Islamic banks to develop. By 1995, a total of 144 Islamic financial institutions had been set up worldwide, including 40 private banks and 33 state-operated banks. Some, such as the now-disbanded Islamic Bank International of Denmark, were connected to specific organizations, in this case the Muslim Brotherhood. Others merely formed mechanisms for pious investments, licit mortgage lending, or funding the burgeoning number of Islamic charities.

After 9/11, American authorities orchestrated a clampdown on the financial enablers of various Islamic political organizations. But global Islamic charities continued to expand as modern vehicles for the core Muslim duty of *zakat* (almsgiving) to the poor.

Multiple choices for the millennial generation

By the early twenty-first century, the multiple Salafi and Deobandi organizations that had emerged over the previous half century had achieved an extraordinary global reach, both in their political and nonpolitical versions. But there were now many more competitors from different regions seeking to catch up with the longer

Indo-Pakistani and Saudi-Egyptian input into global Islam, not least those based in Europe.

While Salafi and Deobandi organizations sought to redefine the religiosity of Muslim-heritage migrants in the West, the sheer variety of people on the move by the 2000s drew increasing numbers of Islamic organizations into the competition to evangelize them. The Turkish migrant presence in Germany, for example, attracted representatives of a variety of different versions of Islam from Turkey. These ranged from traditional Kurdish Alevism and the modernist Hizmet/Gülen movement to the political activism of the Millî Görüş (National Vision) and the Adalet ve Kalkınma Partisi (Justice and Development Party), an Islamic political party founded 2001. While Millî Görüş encouraged Muslims to separate themselves from Western culture, Hizmet promoted a very different vision of Islam. Exiled to the United States since 1999, its leader, Fethullah Gülen, devoted his many Western-oriented interviews to the necessity on a globalized planet of religious tolerance and interfaith dialogue. Nonetheless, in 2013 claims of its political ambitions saw his organization banned and then persecuted in Turkey itself.

The sheer variety of competing versions of global Islam now present in the diaspora was politically and existentially perplexing for Muslims and non-Muslims alike. As Western governments rushed to find "representatives" of their Muslim minorities in the wake of 9/11, the long-standing strategy of Salafi organizations to position themselves as mediators between the state and minorities within it enabled them to gain considerable influence among non-Muslim officials in defining Islam and state policies toward it. Salafi organizations also gained influence among Western Muslims themselves without necessarily promoting the violence that was distinct to Salafi-jihadist subgroups. In some cases, this came through their ability to channel anger at Western intervention in Afghanistan and Iraq through the foundational Salafi narrative of Muslim oppression by the Western powers.

Yet for many second-generation Western Muslims, Salafism also offered a comprehensible moral alternative to both soulless Western consumerism and the seemingly irrelevant world Islam of their parents' unfamiliar homelands. On satellite television and, increasingly, online, preachers such as Yusuf al-Qaradawi presented Salafi Islam as an easy, natural, and universal form of religious practice based on the ethical, behavioral, and even sartorial codes of the Prophet Muhammad's first followers.

Another Salafi vehicle was the English translation of the Quran made by the prominent Moroccan Salafi Taqi al-Din al-Hilali and the Pakistani Muhammad Muhsin Khan (b. 1927). In 1994, the King Fahd Complex for Printing the Holy Quran issued a mass edition of the Hilali-Khan translation, enlarged to 2,000 pages by means of notes and appendices, for free distribution throughout the English-speaking world. Dozens more editions followed in European, African, and Asian languages, while vast numbers of Chinese translations were distributed through new mosques built in China. Since these free Qurans allowed many believers to access the revelation in their own language for the first time, Hilali's commentary could not wholly control how they would interpret the Quran. Increased access to the scripture allowed Muslims to form their own opinions of its meaning and, in so doing, to reject the readings of Salafis no less than other authorities.

Salafis were in any case by no means the sole religious suppliers to the Muslim populations of Europe and the Americas. By the 2000s, an increasing variety of organizations were presenting different versions of Islam for Western Muslims to choose from. Salafis were more deeply entrenched than their Sufi competitors in Islamic institutions in the West. But some Sufi masters recognized the need to catch up by forming organizational replacements to their traditional *tariqas* (brotherhoods). After facing opposition from Salafi organizations in Lebanon, the Sufi-inspired Jam'iyyat al-Mashari al-Khayriyya al-Islamiyya (Association of Islamic Charitable Projects) established branches

10. The transformation from world Islam to global Islam is captured in these two mosques in China: the one above, in traditional style, in Xi'an (built 1392), and the one below, in Saudi style, in Shadian (built 2009).

in North America and eastern Europe, where it took advantage of the "new Europe" to gain a considerable following in Ukraine, as well as central and Southeast Asia. Better known as al-Ahbash (The Ethiopians), this blend of Sufi brotherhood and NGO emerged among Sunni and Shi'i followers of Abdullah al-Harari (1906–2008), a highly educated Sufi who had settled in Beirut in 1950 after being exiled from Ethiopia. By 2011, his organization's itinerary had come full circle as the Ethiopian government tried to promote al-Ahbash as an alternative to the Salafi-Wahhabism that Saudi Arabia was promoting across Africa.

Other new forms of Sufi organization were also taking shape, sometimes with state support. In response to the electoral victory of a party promoting political Islam in Algeria, back in 1991 the government had established the Association Nationale des Zawiyas (National Association of Sufi Lodges). The association subsequently sought to promote Sufi Islam among the Algerian diaspora in Europe. As a similar counter to political Islam, with Moroccan government patronage the Boutchichia Sufi brotherhood, led by Hamza al-Qadiri al-Boutchichi (1922–2017), gained thousands of Arab-heritage followers in Europe. After socialist South Yemen collapsed in 1990, suppressed Sufi leaders reemerged in its Hadramawt region, opening new seminaries such as Dar al-Mustafa (House of the Elected One), founded in 1997. Under the leadership of Sayyid Habib Omar (b. 1963), this Sufi college attracted a small but dedicated student cohort from as far away as Africa, Indonesia, and the United States.

In the 2000s, Minhaj-ul-Quran International, a Sufi-inspired organization founded in Pakistan in 1980 by Muhammad Tahir-ul-Qadri (b. 1951), similarly spread via the Pakistani diasporas in the Gulf and Europe. Its members tried to theologically undermine violent revolutionary forms of global Islam. Yet as its name—meaning "Method of the Quran"— suggests, it has had to resort to Salafi terms for its defense of Sufi teachings. Other new transnational Sufi-inspired organizations established themselves in such unexpected regions as Argentina and Mexico. One was the Movimiento Mundial Murabitun (Murabitun World Movement), founded by the Scottish convert Abdalqadir as-Sufi (born Ian Dallas in 1930). Having first encountered Sufism in Morocco, he went on to establish a following in Spain, which in turn enabled his Latin American outreach.

While many such new Sufi organizations moved across the open borders of the early twenty-first century, none could match the level of state and institutional support acquired by their various Salafi, Wahhabi, and Deobandi antagonists, or the political Shi'ism promoted by the Islamic Republic of Iran. After Saudi Arabia funded the Centro Cultural Islámico Rey Fahd of Buenos Aires, completed in 2001 as Latin America's largest mosque, Iran promptly founded three Shi'i mosques in Argentina. Whether in Latin America or elsewhere, Sufi groups had no petrodollar patrons, no international brokers like the Muslim World League, no network of universities across Africa and Asia, and no system of alliances like the Federation of Islamic Organizations in Europe.

However tacit, the alliance of some Sufi organizations with autocratic governments in Morocco, Algeria, Egypt, and Chechnya weakened their moral authority, as Salafi critics made clear. By contrast, Salafi organizations such as the Muslim Brotherhood openly protested against such regimes.

Global Islam goes online

By the early twenty-first century, the organization- and state-based infrastructure that had shaped the contours of global Islam for the past half century faced new challenges as alternative means of propagation emerged, first via satellite television and then via the Internet.

Initially, the high costs associated with satellite television favored large-scale private and state religious organizations. Al Jazeera, for example, was funded by the Qatari state as a counter to Iran's various state-sponsored Shi'i satellite channels, as well as their private Shi'i counterparts such as al-Anwar (Divine Lights), financed by Kuwaiti Shi'i businessmen. However, the rise first of the Internet and then of the smartphone saw the costs of global propagation fall dramatically. A generation after the rise of Islamic states, this allowed a whole new range of individual religious activists to emerge who challenged the authority of Islamic states and organizations alike.

Even so, the Islamic Republic of Iran and the Muslim Brotherhood were hardly willing to stand by and watch as the digital revolution washed away their authority. Nor were secular authoritarian regimes. As a result, the virtual world created by online Islam became a space of fierce contestation—a "splinternet"—in which states, organizations, and individual activists competed to control the powerful symbolic repertoires made available by the audiovisual possibilities of online communication. The printed journals of the previous two periods were increasingly challenged by more emotionally persuasive combinations of verbal rhetoric and visual imagery.

Despite the aura of cultural authenticity that characterized Islamic satellite television and Internet content, their presentational and fundraising models were taken in part from the American Christian televangelists who broadcast across large parts of Asia and Africa. After Al Jazeera began broadcasting in 2006, the Qatar-based Egyptian theologian Yusuf al-Qaradawi, an admirer of Maududi and al-Banna, became the world's most visible Salafi through his weekly program *Sharia and Life*. By contrast, the Egyptian Amr Khaled (b. 1967), a former accountant with a doctorate in Islamic studies from Wales, broadcast critiques of political Islam from the Arab world's earlier media hub in

Cairo. His hugely popular programs had names such as *Da'wat al-Ta'aish* (Call for Coexistence).

Meanwhile, from India's media center in Mumbai, in 2006 Zakir Naik (b. 1965) used his Islamic Research Foundation to found Peace TV, which by 2015 was broadcasting in nine languages. Despite promoting a scripturalist version of Islam that helped him win Saudi Arabia's King Faisal International Prize, his lack of formal religious qualifications (he was a medical doctor by training) saw Deoband's central *madrasa* issue a *fatwa* forbidding people to listen to him. But the *ulama* were overruled in the online court of popular opinion: by 2017 Naik's Facebook page had over 16 million "likes." Advertised online, his writings were stocked by Muslim booksellers in regions as far removed as India and Bosnia.

Beginning in 2005, the creation first of social media and then of handheld devices offered even newer possibilities of outreach. Existing religious organizations certainly joined the move online, with the likes of the wholly different Aga Khan Foundation and Taliban both investing in digital outreach. Among the most successful websites was IslamOnline.net, which, in its offices in Cairo, Qatar, and Washington, DC, soon employed nearly 200 full-time and 2,000 part-time contributors. Available in English and Arabic, the site was reportedly connected to Qatar's Al-Balagh Cultural Society, in which till 2010 the leading Salafi Yusuf al-Qaradawi played a leading role. However, traditionalist *ulama* and Sufis also took to the Internet, albeit usually with far fewer staff. A notable exception were the wealthy Shi'i institutions around the Iraqi *marja' al-taqlid* (model for emulation), Ali al-Sistani (b. 1930). Among many charitable activities, the religious taxes collected from Sistani's followers funded an abundant online presence in Arabic, Persian, Turkish, Urdu, French, and of course English.

Even as such established religious authorities made use of the digital revolution, its disruptive effects empowered many upstart individual religious entrepreneurs at their expense. By 2015, a decade after the founding of YouTube, hundreds of solo cybermissionaries were expounding hybrid blends of scripture and science, identity politics and conspiracy theories, with little or no precedent in the fourteen centuries of Islamic tradition. The digitized democratization of access to global communication via YouTube, Telegram and similar platforms gave powerful tools to radical revolutionaries and their liberal Muslim critics alike.

Among the latter was Hamza Yusuf (b. 1958). An American convert, Yusuf studied Sufism in Britain, then Arabic in the United Arab Emirates, before founding his Zaytuna Institute (named after the olive branch of peace) in Berkeley, California, in 1996. An early adapter of the West Coast's new technologies, by 2020 Yusuf's online lectures had 85,000 YouTube subscribers.

The Internet not only held a digital magnifying mirror to the fragmentation of global Islam in the physical world; it also provided an accelerating engine for the longer process of divorcing Muslims from their traditions and authorities and promoting new ones in their stead. This was seen most visibly in the rapid ascent of an organization that the overwhelming majority of Muslims viewed with repugnance: the Islamic State of Iraq and Syria.

The disruptive innovations of ISIS

Amid the destruction wrought by the US and British invasion of Iraq, ISIS effectively harnessed the religiously disruptive forces of the digital revolution.

The sheer horror of Iraq at the height of the war fed into a messianic theology that ISIS promoted through sophisticated use of Telegram, Twitter, and Facebook. For its youthful recruits (some of whom were British, American, and Australian converts), its uncensored online content was more visually and politically appealing than the moderate sermons of state-surveilled mosques. Amid the brief heyday of uncensored Internet freedom, ISIS was a vividly extreme example of the blend of religious entrepreneurship, proselytizing innovation, and transnational recruitment that globalization's latest digital toolkit made possible. Until the loss of its last territories in March 2019 and the suicide of its founder seven months later, it deployed a novel combination of the recruitment-generating virtual space of the Internet and the revenue-generating tangible space of Syria and Iraq.

Even so, with its caliphate led by a farmer's son empowered by a PhD from the Islamic University of Baghdad, ISIS was also the heir to the previous half-century's proliferation of revolutionary ideas and new educational routes to religious authority. Moreover, ISIS was an audacious manipulator of the language of authenticity: it resurrected the title of caliph, or *khalifa* (successor of the Prophet), which had lain unclaimed since the dissolution of the Ottoman Empire in 1924. In a distorted echo of the *bay'at* (pledges) given to the first caliphs of Islam, the ISIS leader Abu Bakr al-Baghdadi was able to gain the allegiance of groups as far away as central Africa, the Philippines, and Sri Lanka, where April 2019 witnessed ISIS's worst extraterritorial act of violence.

The media magnification of ISIS, like that of al-Qaeda before it, not only helped inspire Western fear of Islam; it also inspired new Islamic organizations elsewhere to adopt violence as a strategy of gaining influence through coercion rather than persuasion. This was seen in Africa's vast Sahel region, where the likes of Boko Haram (Western Education Is Forbidden), Ansar al-Din (Supporters of Religion), and Al-Mourabitoun (The Sentinels) used spectacular violence to expand their activities across Libya, Nigeria, Cameroon, Chad, Mali, Niger, Burkina Faso, and the Central African Republic, as well as Somalia and southward into Mozambique. Many of their targets were the Sufi shrines that formed the institutional anchors of Africa's traditional world Islam. While ISIS drew much of its funding from captured oil wells, its counterparts in the Sahel have relied on capturing or "taxing" the region's booming gold mines. Despite media attention to terrorist attacks in Europe, the vast majority of the victims have been other Muslims or, in Nigeria, African Christians.

Nowhere were the conflicts between rival versions of Islam more visible than in the war in Syria, which after beginning in 2011 as an internal conflict soon escalated into a transnational sectarian struggle in which ISIS was only one player. Building on the global networks formed a generation earlier during the Afghan jihad, the war in Syria attracted self-designated mujahidin from Sunni and Shi'i communities worldwide. By 2015, the United Nations estimated the number of "foreign terrorist fighters" in Syria at more than 25,000 individuals from over 100 different countries. Among the various Sunni fighting units, Jabhat al-Nusra (al-Nusra Front) was commanded by a Uyghur veteran from Afghanistan. Echoing Sunni transnational recruitment, Shi'i combatants included Iranian Revolutionary Guards, Lebanese Hizbullah, the Fatemiyoun Brigade of Afghan Hazaras, and the Zainabiyoun Brigade from Pakistan. This was a stark contrast to the state of affairs a century earlier, when the Ottoman Empire's attempt to promote a transnational jihad during the First World War had foundered for lack of support.

Such jihadist organizations counted only a tiny proportion of the world's Muslims as members. Yet the communicational and financial toolkit of globalization had enabled them to gain visibility and influence to the disproportionate point that they were affecting geopolitics worldwide.

State-level responses were complex and at times contradictory. At the same time Islamic states such as Iran and Saudi Arabia were funding rival groups fighting in Syria, they tried to rein in organizations they had once funded. In secular autocracies such as

Egypt, the state-appointed Sufi rector of al-Azhar, Ahmed el-Tayeb (b. 1946), used his position as head of the world's most famous traditional Sunni *madrasa* to denounce ISIS, the Muslim Brotherhood, and Salafism in general. Other Muslim-majority autocracies sponsored global congresses to build support networks between Sufi representatives of traditional world Islam, such as the International Sufi Conference in Mostagenem, Algeria, and the International Conference on Sunni Islam in Grozny, Chechnya, both in 2016. After ISIS struck in Turkey, the latter's authoritarian government similarly promoted the Menzil-Naqshbandi Sufi brotherhood. For their part, Western democracies scrambled to promote religious leaders drawn from Islam's peaceful silent majority while at the same time expanding antijihadist military operations into sub-Saharan Africa and Libya.

Yet, as the third era of global Islam drew to a close in 2020, certain developments hinted at a new chapter of history, in which global Islam would assume different shapes and trajectories. ISIS, the most extreme version of the several Islamic states that had emerged in the past half century, had surrendered its last territory. Omar al-Bashir, who had ruled Sudan as an Islamic state since 1989 and previously hosted al-Qaeda, was overthrown in 2019 by his own citizens. Disillusionment with neoliberal globalization was leading various countries to promote nationalist policies, most assertively with China's brutal Sinicization campaign but also in several Muslim-majority states. Surveys suggested that the Arab public in the Middle East was increasingly rejecting the promoters of political Islam who had risen during previous decades. For its part, Saudi Arabia stopped funding European mosques and banned the Muslim Brotherhood, while its crown prince Mohammad bin Salman (b. 1985) pledged to use state resources to promote what he called *"al-islam al-mut'adil wa al-munfatah"* ("a moderate and open Islam"). As the coronavirus crisis of 2020 ushered in a retraction from previous decades of globalization, even the Haram Mosque around the Kaaba in

Mecca remained closed throughout Ramadan with no overseas visitors allowed to perform that year's *hajj*.

Across the period between 1970 and 2020 as a whole, political and technological developments enabled a bewildering number of new Islamic religious actors to emerge at a global level. Around the globe, states, organizations, and individual online activists promulgated a cacophony of competing and often contradictory versions of Islam. The overall outcome was the paradox of Islam in the twenty-first century. Islam has become far more globally visible than at any point in its history. But the fragmentation of religious authority—especially among the Sunni majority—has made it increasingly difficult to define what Islam actually teaches without hearing a contradictory counterclaim. Yet the wide range of Islamic thought also has strong traditions of reconciliation and cohabitation. The future may bring resolution rather than further conflict.

Conclusions

As defined in this book, global Islam comprises the different forms of Islam disseminated by activists, organizations, and states that made effective use of the mechanisms of globalization. This means that global Islam is neither the sum nor the outcome of fourteen centuries of Islamic tradition. Rather, it is the result of attempts to reform, reject or occasionally recover such traditions in response to a century and a half of intense interaction with non-Muslim states, societies, ideas, and institutions.

This formative role of Muslim contact with a wider world explains why so often global Islamic organizations emerged from cities with connections to the widest transregional networks, often as the legacy of imperial globalization. Urban centers in Egypt, India, Pakistan, and Saudi Arabia have thus contributed more as religious exporters than Africa and central Asia, which generally acted more in the role of religious importers. Yet as different world regions were opened and closed to the forces of globalization, European cities also became hubs of global Islam. The absence of long-established Muslim populations in western Europe (and North America) meant that global Islamic organizations faced far less competition there from existing Islamic religious establishments than they did in their original homelands. During the mid-twentieth century, meanwhile, older Muslim regions in central Asia and China fell into abeyance before being reconnected—and in some measure reconverted—during the borderless decades of neoliberalism. Thus, global Islam has never reached everywhere at the same time, but has instead been distributed in accordance with the vacillations of globalization in general.

Yet geography accounts for only some aspects of the evolution of global Islam. Equally important were the strategies adopted, first by transnational activists, then by the organizations that emerged from or moved into such globalized regions, and finally by the policies of various Islamic states or political parties. Over and again, communicational and organizational choices shaped the relative success of different religious actors. Generally speaking, the most effective Islamic globalizers adapted a variety of new communication technologies from the non-Muslim contexts in which they had originally developed. Gradually, the new media of global Islam expanded from print to television and the Internet, all of which involved an increasing use of vernacular languages along with the Muslim lingua francas of English and Arabic.

Underlying these new propagational media were a variety of infrastructures—postal systems, steamship networks, telegraph cables, radio transmitters, television satellites, fiber-optic cables—constructed mainly by the non-Muslim societies that dominated the modern world economy. As a result, global Islam found expression in genres with little or no precedent in Islamic tradition, whether missionary magazines, newspaper articles, Quran translations, cassette sermons, satellite televangelism, or YouTube videos. Only a small proportion of the traditional heritage of world Islam was transferred into these new media, such that the older written teachings of Sufi Islam were increasingly disregarded in fragile and forgotten manuscripts with no mechanisms of circulation or translation. In this way, the transformation of the enabling media of Islam involved not only the promotion of new ideas and actors, but also the demotion of old ones.

The adaptive process that shaped communicational changes also effected organizational changes, as the most successful global Islamic actors learned to adapt techniques from non-Muslim role models. The latter included Christian missionary societies, international congresses, socialist trade unions, Marxist revolutionary cells, paramilitary units, secular universities, pressure groups, NGOs, and charities. The sheer scale of these communicational and organizational adaptations is testament to the "globalized" character of global Islam as the outcome of interactions and exchanges with the wider world.

During Europe's imperial heyday, such was the vivid contrast between a powerful non-Muslim "West" and a weak Islamic "East" that many new Islamic activists rejected traditional world Islam as the underlying cause of Muslim weakness. At the same time, the traditional Sufi-*ulama* who had long comprised the religious authorities proved less successful in making crucial communicational, organizational, and doctrinal adaptations to a rapidly changing world. In part, this was because they had long enjoyed a dominant (often hereditary) "establishment" position that discouraged them from wholesale organizational reinvention and the communicational and fundraising possibilities it brought with it.

By contrast, their anti-Sufi opponents were forced to become more entrepreneurial in their pursuit of followers, emerging as they did as antiestablishment upstarts: a strikingly high proportion of the men who founded transnational journals and organizations had no background in the *madrasas* or Sufi brotherhoods that formed the traditional routes to religious authority. Although some Sufi masters did subsequently find transnational followings, there emerged no Sufi counterweight to the Muslim Brotherhood or the Tablighi Jamaat, nor did Sufi-*ulama* control any of the Islamic states that emerged in the later twentieth century.

Sociological changes also led the older world Islam of the Sufis to fall out of favor with more educated and scientifically aware urban citizens, whose cities were easily reached by different promoters of global Islam. As time progressed, an increasing proportion of the world's Muslims lived in such interconnected cities. By the mid-twentieth century, modernizing nationalist, socialist, and finally Islamic states subsidized the activities of many anti-Sufi organizations that further undermined the former religious establishments. The result was that in terms of publishing, teaching, and other forms of *da'wa* (propagation), a broad spectrum of newer Salafi and Deobandi organizations far outreached the older Sufi brotherhoods. Inadvertently, the socialist destruction of Sufi institutions and organizations across the Soviet Union, southeastern Europe, China, and parts of the Middle East and Africa further paved the way for Salafis and Tablighis when the socialist order crumbled.

As a consequence, global Islam increasingly diverged from the older forms of world Islam, which its promoters often viewed with disdain. This tension with the older heritage of world Islam even characterized some Sufi masters, who replaced traditional shrine veneration and miracle cures with a heightened emphasis on the Quran or adaptations of Western psychology. Such changes brought about a gradual redefining of the realm of religious possibility. This still leaves enormous room for doctrinal variation. But the widespread use of printing and translation saw global Islam's terms of doctrinal reference become increasingly textual and scriptural, as well as scientific, citing Quran and Hadith rather than following the local rituals or miracle-working holy men of world Islam. From the Balkans to India and China, the old Persian Sufi classics were dropped from syllabi they had dominated for centuries. This should not necessarily be a cause for regret or nostalgia: it was in many cases the cultural cost of mass education and the reconciling of religion with modernity.

Nonetheless, by the early twenty-first century, the combined critiques of scripturalist and rationalist reformers had changed the terms of doctrinal reference even for Sufi defenders of world Islam. This brings us to what is perhaps the central paradox of global Islam. Easier access to the communicational toolkit of globalization has created an ever-increasing number of rival religious activists, organizations, and states. But at the same time, the theological, ritual, and legal parameters of what constitutes Islam have contracted in response to the competitive polemics generated by these proliferating claims to religious authority.

Simply put, for all their rivalry, the various promoters of global Islam broadly agree in rejecting as *khurafat* (superstitions) or *bid'at* (innovations) the sacred sites, carnivals, local customs, and ritual paraphernalia that for centuries formed the regional expressions of world Islam. For many Muslims this rejection is the reasonable price of being modern. But it nonetheless testifies to the religious transformations that global Islam has disseminated.

And so, since the onset of modern globalization around 1870 global Islam has increasingly diverged from the older forms of Islam that its promoters have sought to reform or replace. This metapattern of divergence has taken shape alongside a second metapattern of fragmentation, witnessed in the ever-increasing number of religious activists, organizations, and states that compete for religious authority. This social reality stands in stark contrast to the calls for Muslim unity that have characterized global Islam since its origin and have survived through the enduring discursive influence of the Ottoman campaign for Islamic unity.

Since the late nineteenth century, globalization has led to increasing calls for religious unity and conformity as greater inter-Muslim communication heightened awareness of Muslim diversity and disunity, particularly in the face of Western hegemony. But as different religious actors with varying agendas called for unity on different terms, the effect was to generate further disunity and diversification through the creation of more and more organizations and then states, each claiming to present the true version of Islam. Thus, in the course of a century and a half, wider access to the organizational and communicational toolkit of globalization fueled the dissolution of religious authority as more and more religious actors sought to redefine Islam on their own terms.

Consequently, globalization has not resulted in Muslim unification. Rather, it has led to increasing religious fragmentation as more and more activists, organizations, and states compete for the right to define Islam, albeit usually within more confined scripturalist and rationalist parameters than those recognized by world Islam. Since the late twentieth century, the falling costs of digital communication have radically lowered the barriers of entry to Islam's fractious global religious marketplace even further.

Yet such fragmentation has not prevented different organizations from at times working together toward common goals. This development has been most prominently seen in the connected campaigns in many countries since the 1970s for the expansion of Sharia, as well as in transnational protests against "blasphemy," whether committed by European cartoonists or South Asian novelists. In each case, these are outcomes of the increased awareness and interaction made possible by global communications. Whether such increased awareness will ever overcome the dynamic that is propelling fragmentation remains to be seen. Globalization can, after all, produce multiple and countervailing trajectories.

These countervailing trajectories may be seen in the complex dynamics that have led some *ulama* and Sufi masters to respond to the assault on their authority by forming their own newly reformed doctrines and methods of outreach, which produce further fragmentation in turn. While the disintegration of religious authority has particularly affected Sunni Islam, in Shi'i contexts, by contrast, the toolkit of globalization was used to centralize authority around the handful of senior *ulama* recognized as a *marja' al-taqlid* (authority to be followed), then around the Supreme Leader of the Islamic Republic of Iran. Among Ismaili Shi'is, globalization similarly enabled the centralization of religious authority around the Aga Khan and Bohra *da'i*. While none of these cases of Shi'i centralization was wholly successful—there was also a countervailing trajectory of new Shi'i leaders who rejected the *ulama*, imam, and *da'i*—the broad distinction between Sunni and Shi'i trajectories demonstrates that globalization does not possess an innate teleology. Rather, it suggests that different actors can manage globalization to different effects.

In the new period of history ushered in by the onset of the coronavirus pandemic in 2020, Muslim religious activists, organizations, and states will learn to manage as best they can the changing conditions created by the contraction of globalization. While prediction is a precarious venture, their methods will likely draw on those that emerged from the three preceding eras of waxing and waning globalization.

In concluding, it is important to recognize the limits of the analysis offered here. The focus has been deliberately confined to what might be termed the "supply side" of religion, that is, activists, organizations, and states. This has left out of the picture the "demand side": the ordinary people who follow—or, indeed, reject—the religious orientations presented by such "suppliers". A truly holistic (albeit much longer) analysis of global Islam would necessarily consider both sides of the equation and in doing so tackle the question of why the messages of particular global Islamic organizations appeal to particular groups of Muslims. Yet this question of the appeal and reception of global Islam requires careful sociological inquiries into the multiple local settings where different organizations have been active. So far, pioneering research into these many worldwide settings is too patchy and incomplete to make responsible generalizations. Future investigations of the many points where the global meets the local will likely reveal many different reasons for following, or rejecting, different versions of global Islam that reflect variable social, political, economic, educational, and cultural circumstances. By contrast, what we have seen here is a more confined sketch of the global religious actors that have reached into those myriad local environments and the mechanisms that have enabled them to do so.

Global Islam is not synonymous with the faith and practice of the world's Muslims as a whole. By way of analogy, recognizing that evangelical and Pentecostal organizations have been the most successful Christian globalizers in recent decades is not the same as saying that the majority of the world's Christians belong to such churches. It is important to emphasize that perhaps hundreds of millions of Muslims still follow some version of their traditional world Islam. And recognizing that Sufi Islam has been less successful than its alternatives is not to imply that global Islam is uniformly dominated by "extremists" or "fundamentalists." Anti-Sufi reformers often had good reason for their critiques of wealthy and hereditary Sufi leaders, while the reformist spectrum includes many nonpolitical as well as political theologies, with only some of the latter supporting violence.

Nor should global Islam be seen as simplistically representative of the varied beliefs and opinions of Muslim-heritage populations in the West, who include many skeptics, secularists, and, increasingly, atheists. And while some forms of global Islam evolved as direct challenges to the West, others were developed as means of accommodating Muslims to either life as pious minorities or dominant secular modernity, while protecting them from the moral pitfalls of Western lifestyles. Other global Islamic projects evolved as religious responses to grave dilemmas ranging from Arab autocracy to African poverty, situations for which Western solutions were not self-evidently superior. In other cases, most notably the anti-Soviet jihad, Western policies aligned with and empowered those of global Islamic groups.

Since the active promoters of global Islam comprise only a small proportion of the world's Muslim population, the spread of global Islam is not a simple reflection of the demographic power of numbers. On the contrary, global Islam has been produced and distributed by small but active minorities, albeit minorities who are able to make maximum use of the power of networks, communications, and, in some cases, state policies and resources. It would therefore be a mistake to simplistically extrapolate the beliefs and opinions of the world's highly diverse Muslim populations on the basis of a series of unelected religious organizations, however much the latter have claimed to represent ordinary Muslim opinion.

All over the world, millions of Muslims have already recognized, reckoned with, and rejected the ways in which their religion has become entangled with globalization and geopolitics. In response, many have developed personal, local, and in some cases national-level alternatives to the global forms of Islam that emerged far from the places where they pass their lives. While these little-studied responses to global Islam are not the subject of this book, they may become more influential in future decades.

The focus here has not, then, been on all the world's Muslims or on the local community activists and national organizations that have tried to resist global Islamic trends by promoting national Islamic identities and local interfaith solidarities. What we have seen are the communicational and organizational processes that enabled some versions of Islam to cross political and ethnolinguistic boundaries more effectively than others. This was an incremental process in which each fifty-year phase contributed its doctrinal and organizational legacy to the next, in a sequence that grew from individual activists to transnational organizations to Islamic states. It is ultimately this process that explains the heightened global visibility of Islam in the twenty-first century.

Glossary

Bid‘a (**pl.** *bid‘at*): "Innovation"; term used to condemn practices not recorded in the Quran or Hadith (q.v.)

Da‘i: Hereditary leader of the Bohra branch of Ismaili Shi‘ism

Da‘iya (**pl.** *du‘at*): A Muslim missionary

Da‘wa: Muslim religious propagation

Hadith: "Reports"; traditions of the sayings and deeds of the Prophet and his early followers (and for Shi‘is, also the imams, q.v.)

Hajj: The pilgrimage to Mecca

Hisba: "Forbidding wrong and commanding good"; core Salafi doctrine that encourages denunciation of non-Salafi (especially Sufi and Shi‘i) Muslims

Imam: "Leader"; a prayer leader (among Sunnis); descendants of the Prophet's family who form infallible leaders (among Shi‘is)

Ismaili: Minority Shi‘i communities who follow the Aga Khan or Bohra *da‘i* (q.v.) as their imam (q.v.)

Khanaqah: A traditional Sufi meeting house

Mab‘uth (**pl.** *mab‘uthun*): A Muslim missionary (preferred term of the Muslim World League)

Madrasa: A Muslim religious seminary

Marja‘ al-Taqlid: Authority to be followed; highest-ranking Shi‘i clerics

Mujahidin: Those who partake in holy war (*jihad*)

Shaykh: "Elder"; title of respect for Sufi masters or senior *ulama* (q.v.)

Sharia: "The Way"; religious law formulated through interpretation of the Quran and Hadith (q.v.)

Sufi: Initiate of a Sufi master or brotherhood that teaches mystical practices and channels the miraculous blessing power of the Prophet

Sufi-*ulama*: Traditional religious leaders who combine the authority of a Sufi lineage and *madrasa* education

Sunna: "The Model"; body of exemplary traditions drawn from the life of the Prophet

Tabligh: Religious propagation; missionary work

Twelver Shi'i: The largest of Shi'ism's several denominations, forming the majority population of Iran, Iraq, and Bahrain, with minorities elsewhere. Named after their lineage of twelve imams (q.v.)

Ulama: "The learned"; those who have mastered scripture, law, and other normative subjects, usually in a *madrasa* (q.v.)

References

Chapter 2

For publication statistics in the Ottoman Empire, see
Jacob M. Landau, *The Politics of Pan-Islam: Ideology and
Organization* (Oxford: Oxford University Press, 1990), 58.

Chapter 3

On Muslim Brotherhood–affiliated organizations in Europe and the
United States, see Lorenzo Vidino, *The New Muslim Brotherhood
in the West* (New York: Columbia University Press, 2010), 27–55.

Chapter 4

For statistics on Pakistani *madrasas* founded during the 1980s, see
David Commins, *The Mission and the Kingdom: Wahhabi Power
behind the Saudi Throne* (London: Bloomsbury, 2016), 191.
On the number of African countries to which the Islamic University of
Madinah sent representatives, see Michael Farquhar, *Circuits of
Faith: Migration, Education, and the Wahhabi Mission* (Palo Alto,
CA: Stanford University Press, 2017), 169.
On the number of Nigerian students at the Islamic University of
Madinah, see Alexander Thurston, *Salafism in Nigeria: Islam,
Preaching, and Politics* (Cambridge: Cambridge University Press,
2016), 89.

On the number of Islamic financial institutions founded as of 1995, see Gilles Kepel, *Jihad: The Trail of Political Islam* (London: I. B. Tauris, 2002), 79.

For statistics on Naik's Facebook "likes," see Matthew Kuiper, *Da'wa and Other Religions: Indian Muslims and the Modern Resurgence of Global Islamic Activism* (Abingdon: Routledge, 2017), 183.

On the number of foreign fighters in Syria, see Hamed el-Said and Richard Barrett, *Enhancing the Understanding of the Foreign Terrorist Fighters Phenomenon in Syria* (New York: United Nations Office of Counter-Terrorism, 2017), 3.

For statistics on the Arab public's growing rejection of political Islam in 2019, see the survey by Arab Barometer cited in *The Economist*, December 5, 2019, https://www.economist.com/graphic-detail/2019/12/05/arabs-are-losing-faith-in-religious-parties-and-leaders.

Further reading

Overviews

Green, Nile. *Sufism: A Global History*. Oxford: Wiley–Blackwell, 2012.
Robinson, Francis, ed. *The Cambridge Illustrated History of the Islamic World*. Cambridge: Cambridge University Press, 2002.
Ruthven, Malise. *Islam: A Very Short Introduction*. Oxford: Oxford University Press, 2012.
Steger, Manfred. *Globalization: A Very Short Introduction*. Oxford: Oxford University Press, 2013.

The emergence of global Islam in the age of empire (1870–1920)

Aydin, Cemil. *The Idea of the Muslim World: A Global Intellectual History*. Cambridge, MA: Harvard University Press, 2017.
Gelvin, James L., and Nile Green, eds. *Global Muslims in the Age of Steam and Print*. Berkeley: University of California Press, 2013.
Green, Nile. *Terrains of Exchange: Religious Economies of Global Islam*. New York: Oxford University Press, 2014.
Hassan, Mona. *Longing for the Lost Caliphate: A Transregional History*. Princeton, NJ: Princeton University Press, 2016.
Ingram, Brannon D. *Revival from Below: The Deoband Movement and Global Islam*. Berkeley: University of California Press, 2018.
Laffan, Michael. *Islamic Nationhood and Colonial Indonesia: The Umma below the Winds*. Abingdon: Routledge, 2003.
Landau, Jacob M. *The Politics of Pan-Islam: Ideology and Organization*. Oxford: Oxford University Press, 1990.
Motadel, David, ed. *Islam and the European Empires*. Oxford: Oxford University Press, 2014.

Reese, Scott S. *Imperial Muslims: Islam, Community and Authority in the Indian Ocean, 1839–1937*. Edinburgh: Edinburgh University Press, 2017.

Schayegh, Cyrus, Liat Kozma, and Avner Wishnitzer, eds. *A Global Middle East: Mobility, Materiality and Culture in the Modern Age, 1880–1940*. London: I. B. Tauris, 2014.

Global Islam in the heyday of secular nationalism and socialism (1920–70)

Commins, David. *The Mission and the Kingdom: Wahhabi Power behind the Saudi Throne*. London: Bloomsbury, 2016.

Farquhar, Michael. *Circuits of Faith: Migration, Education, and the Wahhabi Mission*. Palo Alto, CA: Stanford University Press, 2017.

Frampton, Martyn. *The Muslim Brotherhood and the West: A History of Enmity and Engagement*. Oxford: Oxford University Press, 2018.

Fuchs, Simon Wolfgang. *In a Pure Muslim Land: Shi'ism between Pakistan and the Middle East*. Chapel Hill: University of North Carolina Press, 2019.

Kramer, Martin. *Islam Assembled: The Advent of the Muslim Congresses*. New York: Columbia University Press, 1986.

Kuiper, Matthew. *Da'wa and Other Religions: Indian Muslims and the Modern Resurgence of Global Islamic Activism*. Abingdon: Routledge, 2017.

Lauzière, Henri. *The Making of Salafism: Islamic Reform in the Twentieth Century*. New York: Columbia University Press, 2016.

Lipman, Jonathan, ed. *Islamic Thought in China: Sino-Muslim Intellectual Evolution from the 17th to the 21st Century*. Edinburgh: Edinburgh University Press, 2016.

Nordbruch, Götz, and Umar Ryad, eds. *Transnational Islam in Interwar Europe: Muslim Activists and Thinkers*. London: Palgrave Macmillan, 2014.

Piscatori, James P. *Islam in a World of Nation-States*. Cambridge: Cambridge University Press, 1986.

Global Islam in the age of Islamic States, neoliberalism, and the Internet (1970–2020)

Adraoui, Mohamed-Ali. *Salafism Goes Global: From the Gulf to the French Banlieues*. Oxford: Oxford University Press, 2020.

Ahmed, Chanfi. *Preaching Islamic Revival in East Africa*. Cambridge: Cambridge Scholars, 2018.

Balci, Bayram. *Islam in Central Asia and the Caucasus since the Fall of the Soviet Union*. London: Hurst, 2018.

Corboz, Elvire. *Guardians of Shiʿism: Sacred Authority and Transnational Family Networks*. Edinburgh: Edinburgh University Press, 2015.

Jaffrelot, Christophe, and Laurence Louër, eds. *Pan-Islamic Connections: Transnational Networks between South Asia and the Gulf*. New York: Oxford University Press, 2018.

Kepel, Gilles. *Allah in the West: Islamic Movements in America and Europe*. London: Polity Press, 1997.

Maher, Shiraz. *Salafi-Jihadism: The History of an Idea*. Oxford: Oxford University Press, 2016.

Mandaville, Peter. *Global Political Islam*. 2nd ed. Abingdon: Routledge, 2014.

Meijer, Roel, ed. *Global Salafism: Islam's New Religious Movement*. Oxford: Oxford University Press, 2009.

Muedini, Fait. *Sponsoring Sufism: How Governments Promote "Mystical Islam" in Their Domestic and Foreign Policies*. New York: Palgrave Macmillan, 2015.

Piraino, Francesco, and Mark Sedgwick, eds. *Global Sufism: Boundaries, Structures, and Politics*. London: Hurst, 2019.

Rizwi, Kishwar. *The Transnational Mosque: Architecture and Historical Memory in the Contemporary Middle East*. Chapel Hill: University of North Carolina Press, 2015.

Roy, Oliver. *Globalized Islam: The Search for a New Ummah*. New York: Columbia University Press, 2004.

Soares, Benjamin, and René Otayek, eds. *Islam and Muslim Politics in Africa*. New York: Palgrave Macmillan, 2007.

Tahseen Shams, *Here, There, and Elsewhere: The Making of Immigrant Identities in a Globalized World*. Palo Alto, CA: Stanford University Press, 2020.

Thurston, Alexander. *Salafism in Nigeria: Islam, Preaching, and Politics*. Cambridge: Cambridge University Press, 2016.

Zaman, Muhammad Qasim. *The Ulama in Contemporary Islam: Custodians of Change*. Princeton, NJ: Princeton University Press, 2002.

Index